INTRODUCTION TO U.S. LAW AND LEGAL RESEARCH

Dana Neacşu, D.E.A., LL.M., M.L.S.

Transnational Publishers

Published and distributed by *Transnational Publishers, Inc.*
Ardsley Park
Science and Technology Center
410 Saw Mill River Road
Ardsley, NY 10502

Phone: 914-693-5100
Fax: 914-693-4430
E-mail: info@transnationalpubs.com
Web: www.transnationalpubs.com

Library of Congress Cataloging-in-Publication Data

Neacşu, E. Dana.
Introduction to U.S. law and legal research / Dana E. Neacşu.
p. cm.
Includes bibliographical references and index.
ISBN 1-57105-354-9 (casebound)
ISBN 1-57105-358-1 (paperback)
1. Legal research—United States. 2. Law—United States.
I. Title.

KF240.N42 2005
340'.072'073–dc22

2005047147

Contents

Chapter 3
Basic Principles of Legal Research

Chapter 4
Statutory Law: What It Is, Where It Is, and How You Find It

Chapter 5
Case Law: What It Is, Where It Is, and How You Find It

Chapter 6
Administrative Law: What It Is, Where It Is, and How You Find It

Conclusion: Is This All?

Acknowledgments

Co-teaching the introduction to law and legal research aspect of Peter Bower's *Environmental Law And Policy* class at Barnard College, I realized that both undergraduate students, as well as international (LL.M.) students, would benefit from a comprehensive yet introductory text to American law and legal research.

This book was inspired by the intellectually stimulating environment Kent McKeever has successfully encouraged at the Arthur W. Diamond Library, and the generous mentoring Jody Armstrong has provided through her *Advance Legal Research* seminar, which the reference department staff co-teaches at Columbia Law School under her direction. Similarly grateful I am to all my colleagues who have always supported my endeavors, Phil, Karin, Charles, Andrew, and Simon Canick, and especially to Ken Ward, whose friendship I relish every time he visits Columbia to teach his wonderfully provocative political science course on the role of the judiciary. Of course, Mickey, Abby, and Zoe through their assistance, love, and example made it possible for me to thank you all.

D.N.

Foreword

The American Bar Association (ABA) has come to the conclusion that there are "generic types of knowledge that one should possess"[1] at the onset of their legal studies "in order to have a full appreciation of the legal system in general,"[2] and the American legal system, in particular. ABA identifies, *inter alia,* the following fundamental concepts to understanding the American legal system:

> A broad understanding of American history, [. . .]
> A fundamental understanding of political thought and theory, and of the contemporary American political system; [. . .]
> A basic understanding of ethical theory and theories of justice; [. . .][3]

As a guide to where and how you can find the law, *Introduction to U.S. Law and Legal Research* first explains what law is, briefly discussing issues of American legal history, political, and legal thought. The book is valuable to those preparing to pursue a law degree or to answer general questions about law or legal research. As a preparatory tool, *Introduction to U.S. Law and Legal Research* contributes to making your subsequent legal education a more meaningful and manageable process.

---

1 The Pre-Law Committee of the ABA Section of Legal Education and Admissions to the Bar, PRE-LAW. PREPARATION FOR LEGAL EDUCATION *available* at http://www.abanet.org/legaled/prelaw/prep.html#Knowledge.

2 *Id.*

3 *Id.*

Non-Exhaustive Glossary of Terms

Act
An alternative name for statutory law. *See* Statutes.

Action
An alternative name for lawsuit: the process that starts with a demand (through a document named complaint) for state intervention that one party (named plaintiff) makes in order to have her *status quo* restored and the other party (named defendant) punished physically (in a criminal action) or financially (in both criminal and civil action).

Adjudication
The formal ending of a lawsuit by a court and of a dispute by an administrative agency.

Adjudicative Hearings
Proceedings held by administrative agencies similar to trials held in courts of law.

Administrative Agency
A governmental body that issues rules and regulations and even adjudicates disputes between parties, according to powers delegated to it by the legislature (whether federal or state).

Administrative Rules and Regulations
The law issued by (federal or state) administrative agencies according to the powers delegated to them by legislatures that usually further details rules contained in (federal or state) statutes.

Annotations
Brief summaries of court decisions and other editorial explanations that the commercially published codes feature at the end of each statutory section.

Answer
The written document (pleading) the defendant files in response to plaintiff's complaint.

Attorney
Members of a profession regulated by state laws. One of their areas of expertise is to represent other people's legal demands for relief in courts for a fee.

Authority
See Binding Authority and Persuasive Authority

Bill
A legislative proposal that has not been enacted as law.

Binding Authority
The authority statutes command on disputes involving issues within their subject matter, and the authority higher courts decisions have on factually similar disputes brought to lower courts from the same jurisdiction.

Brief

(1) the alternative name for documents that attorneys file in support of their client's legal demands;
(2) a summary of a court's opinion.

Case
See Lawsuit.

Case Law
Alternative name for common law in its narrow meaning of "judge-made law," different from statutory or regulatory law.

Cause of Action
The legal grounds for a civil action.

Citation

(1) reference to authority supporting one's legal argument;
(2) the form used for legal reference.

Civil Law

(1) the other major world legal system (unlike common law it does not officially recognize the precedential value of earlier decisions from higher courts from the same jurisdiction);

(2) the body of law that covers non-criminal matters.

Claim

A formal demand for state redress raised in an action.

Code

(1) a topical compilation of statutes or administrative rules and regulations;

(2) primary source of law.

Common Law

(1) the other major world legal system (unlike civil law it officially recognizes the precedential value of earlier decisions from higher courts from the same jurisdiction);

(2) an alterative name for case law—the body of law that includes only court decisions.

Complaint

The document that starts a civil action.

Constitution

(1) the fundamental law of most national jurisdictions (written or not);

(2) primary source of law.

Controversy

See Lawsuit.

Court Decision

See Judgment and Opinion.

Damages

Monetary compensation ordered by a court to restore plaintiff's *status quo.*

Defendant
The person against whom the plaintiff (the initiating party) brings an action.

Doctrine

(1) a widely accepted legal principle;
(2) the product of writings of professors and other scholars that has a pervasive influence on both the making and application of civil and international law.

Due Process of Law
Constitutional guaranty of a person's enjoyment of her rights provided by the Fifth and 14th Amendment of the United States Constitution.

Hearings
See Adjudicative Hearings and Investigative Hearings.

Holding
The conclusion of law reached by a court in deciding a case or controversy.

Injunction
A court's order that the defendant does or refrains from doing a certain act.

Investigative Hearings
Proceedings held by congressional committees prior to enactment of legislation.

Judgment
The formal conclusion of a case or controversy. *See also* Opinion.

Jurisdiction

(1) the geographical area in which law (in all its forms as court decisions, statutes and administrative rules and regulations) is binding;
(2) the boundaries of authority given to all law-making bodies to make law (decide cases, enact legislation or adopt rules and regulations).

Law

A double-meaning concept:

(1) a human ideal of order and predictability—*see* Rule of Law;

(2) the entire system of rules that materialize that ideal of order and whose enforcement may be state-imposed.

Law Review Articles

One type of secondary sources. Law review articles are usually published by law schools and are student-edited. They contain writings about the law. What distinguishes law review articles from treatises is their narrower scope, its more in depth treatment of the specific legal issue, and its more often acknowledged partisan view.

Lawsuit

A criminal or civil proceeding taking place in a court.

Legislative History

Documents that record the history of a statute from its introduction as a bill sponsored by a legislator to its enactment as a piece of legislation.

Litigate

Asking the state (usually by bringing a lawsuit) to sanction one's demands to restore one's *status quo.*

Litigant

A party to a lawsuit. *See also Pro Se* Litigant.

Motion

A formal request a party to a lawsuit makes to a judge during the lawsuit.

Opinion

The document that records the conclusion reached by a court or administrative agency adjudicating a lawsuit. All court opinions have a well-set structure that contains a heading: the name of the parties, that of their attorneys and the judge issuing the opinion, as well as the name of the court in which the opinion was held down and the date it was pronounced. In addition, court opinions summarize the facts of the case, the legal issues involved in the parties' claims, and the reasons on which the court's conclusions are reached.

Persuasive Authority
The authority case law from other jurisdictions and secondary sources command.

Plaintiff
The person initiating the lawsuit.

Primary Sources
The repository of law, whether it is case law (*e.g.*, reporters), statutes (*e.g.*, codes), or rules and regulations (*e.g.*, codes).

Procedural Law
The body of law that covers the rules governing the administration of justice (the operation of the legal system) as opposed to substantive law, which covers the rules that provide the rights and obligations that enable society to function.

***Pro Se* Litigant**
A party to a lawsuit that has no professional legal representation.

Reporters
(1) primary source;
(2) alternative name for reports;
(3) collections of court decisions, usually arranged loosely by period of time and the court making the decision.

Reports
(1) primary source;
(2) collections of court or administrative agency decisions.

Repository
(1) resource containing primary sources (for example reporters are case-law repositories);
(2) source of individual rights (for example, the Constitution is the repository of our main freedoms).

Rule of Law
A fundamental legal principle of the American legal system.

Secondary Sources
The repository of legal writings about the law that command only persuasive authority (such as law review articles and treatises).

Stare Decisis
Common law principle which states that old cases from higher courts in the same jurisdiction are the bases for new court decisions within the same fact pattern.

Statutes
Acts of a legislature.

Substantive Law
The body of law that covers the rules that provide the rights and obligations that enable society to function, unlike procedural law that cover the rules regarding the administration of justice—how to restore or preserve status quo through litigation of rights and obligations.

Treatise

(1) secondary source;
(2) comprehensive legal writing on an area of law, although less detailed or critical than a law review article.

Writ

(1) the form in which complaints were originally addressed to English courts;
(2) Writ of *certiorari* refers to the discretionary device used by the U.S. Supreme Court to hear cases.

Introduction

> For I think it an undeniable position, that a competent knowledge of the laws of that society, in which we live, is the proper accomplishment of every gentleman and scholar; an highly useful, I had almost said essential, part of liberal and polite education.
>
> *Blackstone's The Study, Nature, and Extent of the Law*

A. THE UBIQUITOUS NATURE OF AMERICAN LAW AND ITS DUAL ROLE OF PRODUCT AND PRODUCER OF POPULAR CULTURE

Whether you study American law outside the United States or intend to enroll in a graduate program in the United States, for an LL.M., you need to become aware of the major differences that exist between your legal system and the U.S. legal system. This book will help you bridge that gap and quickly grasp a solid introductory foundation of American law and legal research techniques that will allow you to easily focus on the legal field of your choice.

When you start studying American law it is useful to be aware of all potential hindrances. Some of them are related to the current nature of American law as both a product and a producer of popular culture, and, as such, students unfamiliar with this aspect of it may fall prey to unfounded assumptions. Its ubiquitous presence in everybody's life causes that many basic explanations about the law be absent from law classes, because American students already have an idea about the bigger picture of the legal system and how it works. On the other hand, such heavy presence may induce you to memorize legal information that comes from sources that lack proper authority, and improperly rely on it, for example, instead of developing a critical approach to legal information.

Other obstacles are related to the origins of American law and the ways in which the sources of American public law create specific legal norms. For example, while, from the outside, the American legal system seems to change very little, the reality is that American law is very dynamic. Its dynamism relies on a rhetoric of individual rights that perhaps is little known to you.

Additionally, while American students know that the federal structure of the American government is mirrored by the legal system, you may not be familiar with the American political system. Thus, it may be easier for native American students to understand that federal and state laws are not covered by one source of law, but instead such laws are located in distinct repositories of statutory and decisional law, whether at the federal or state level. Thus, becoming familiar with these idiosyncrasies of American law is a prerequisite to both successful legal studies and research.

In other countries, interest in law usually surfaces at times of political crises. For example, it is understandable that political circumstances of this time make exposure to law a daily occurrence. The fact that America was attacked and is currently engaged in military action raises legal issues that ask for everybody's opinion and understanding. For example, John Walker Lindh, an American citizen, fought for the Taliban, while knowing that the United States was engaged in hostilities against the Taliban. Looking beyond one's gut feelings, can we define his actions as treason? Is there a definition of treason under the U.S. legal system? Where can it be found: in a compilation of federal statutes or in a reporter of Supreme Court cases? How can it be located? (See Fig. 1.)

However, American law is everywhere today mostly because of its double nature of both a product of popular culture and a creator of popular culture. Whether reading a Grisham novel, watching NBC's "Law and Order," driving faster than the legal speed limit, or drinking McDonalds's hot coffee, law is never far away. You are exposed to law as a product of popular culture—in novels and TV shows—and you are exposed to law as a producer of popular culture. Here, trials of famous people become TV news shows. When

Fig. 1

Treason is defined in the United States Code:

> Whoever, owing allegiance to the United States, levies war against them or adheres to their enemies, giving them aid and comfort within the United States or elsewhere, is guilty of treason and shall suffer death, or shall be imprisoned not less than five years and fined under this title but not less than $10,000; and shall be incapable of holding any office under the United States.

18 U.S.C. § 2381 (2000).

you watch CNN or Fox News, and you hear the entertainer of the day has just been indicted by the Grand Jury, you are indirectly exposed to law as a producer of popular culture. However, you will be ill-advised to give such knowledge more weight than you would to any other TV shows.

To the extent that American law has become both a product of popular culture and a creator of popular culture, everybody who lives in the United States or studies law in America is exposed to it. As a result, your first encounter with the American law is likely to be mediated:[1] Whether it comes from television and radio broadcasts, newspapers, periodicals, or Internet sites, be aware that like everywhere else, mediated information uses concepts defined according to the views of the show's writers and producers or the creators of the printed material. Thus, faced with the flood of mediated legal information, developing a critical approach to legal information before you start studying law becomes a worth while enterprise.

As an example of American law's dual role as producer and product of popular culture, let's take a look at the film "Monster," which many of you might have seen because it won a 2004 Oscar in the Best Actress category. The movie depicts the life of young

---

1 For a more detailed discussion of law as a product of popular culture and a producer of popular culture, *see* RICHARD K. SHERWIN, WHEN LAW GOES POP: THE VANISHING LINE BETWEEN LAW AND POPULAR CULTURE. (2000).

woman who, in 2002, was convicted and then executed for the killing of seven men. From watching this movie one learns that homicide is defined by each state's law, that the Florida penalty for multiple homicide is the death penalty, and that Florida administers it through lethal injection.

In this instance, law—rules regarding the execution of a convicted felon—produced popular culture—the celebrated movie—and popular culture—the movie—further produced legal knowledge about those issues. Such information may be unreliable. Nevertheless, this shows the extent to which legal knowledge is part of the ordinary Americans' general knowledge. To that extent, you too will benefit from understanding how American law works.

It goes without saying that unless you study American criminal law, such mediated legal knowledge is and remains passive, and it rarely stirs the audience's interest in questioning the legal issues and their outcomes—the crimes at hand and the way American society deals with them. Certainly, it is not intuitive to inquire into the legality of the death penalty although the American constitutional system prohibits inhuman punishment. (See Fig. 2.) That is why just being aware of TV legal shows or printed legal information is not sufficient to bridge the gap between you and the native law student. Reading this introductory book will give you the necessary foundation to develop a critical approach to legal issues on your own.

Of course, you already have considerable legal knowledge. You have studied law within your legal system, and you have encountered law directly and indirectly. Everybody comes in involuntary direct contact with the law at birth, when they become entitled to rights and freedoms automatically, as well as at death when those entitlements end. However, you need to be aware of the extent to which the idea of "legal rights" has become an intrinsic value that is widespread in the American culture. In no other legal system will you encounter this almost religious belief that a rights claim produces a universal and categorical entitlement. The only way to understand the value of such belief is by identifying the right itself,

Fig. 2

Constitutional Amendment VIII. Ratified on 12/15/1791

> Excessive bail shall not be required, nor excessive fines imposed, nor cruel and unusual punishments inflicted.

whether it is mentioned by the Constitution, a statute, or issued by a court, and then by searching its historical interpretation and application by courts.

Furthermore, applying for a driver's license, signing a lease, or marrying, like everybody else, you encounter law directly and voluntarily, too. If you marry within the territory of the United States, the law established by the legislative assembly of each state of the union is binding upon its residents and dictates the minimum ages of the spouses.[2] Or, if you apply for a driver's license, you need to know that each state has its own specific rules, regarding paying a fee and furnishing proofs of identity. Those requirements under New York law are contained both in Vehicle and Traffic Law[3] and in the rules issued by the Commissioner of Motor Vehicles.[4] If you choose to immigrate, you have to follow the statutory provisions set up by the U.S. Congress and the administrative rules issued by the U.S. Citizenship and Immigration Services.

There are a few levels on which this book is designed to help your legal studies. It wants to put to good use all the knowledge you have about law, generally, and about American law, especially.

---

2 Until a few decades ago, laws from many states of the union dictated the race of the married spouses as well; they prohibited U.S. couples of different races from intermarrying. Those statutes were known under the name of "miscegenation laws" and the U.S. Supreme Court declared them unconstitutional in 1966 in a case known as *Loving v. Virginia*, 388 U.S. 1 (1967).

3 N.Y. Veh. & Traf. § 502.

4 *See* N.Y. Comp. Codes R. & Regs. tit. 15, § 7.1 et seq.

Thus, it wants to facilitate your studies of American law and your legal research.

B. WHAT THIS BOOK OFFERS

This book is intended to help you obtain a solid introduction to the complex realm of American law. It brings a critical attitude to your approach of studying and researching legal norms.

Its premise is that you cannot study law if you do not know how to find the law. Like any abstract body of knowledge that rests on both tangible and intangible constructs of human intellect, studying law requires understanding both its abstract and concrete facet. Law is a discourse, a process of power,[5] and tangible norms that make it all possible.

Aside from theology, a body of knowledge about God's word, all the other subjects explain something tangible: whether they are natural or man-made constructs. Linguistics builds on language. Musicology ultimately rests on tangible music sheets.

Legal knowledge builds on the social function of law to ensure social order and stability. This goal is achieved though a myriad of legal norms that govern our social behavior.

The abstract facet of law is far from uniform. It encompasses the ideal of order and predictability as well as the discourse of individual rights, for example. The ideal of order is translated into legitimate order by the requirements imposed by the "rule of law" on the tangible aspect of law—its innumerable norms that constitute different bodies of law, such as torts law, business law, criminal law, or intellectual property law. Studying law rests on understanding the social function of the concrete legal norms, and studying the different bodies of law—torts, intellectual property, etc.—requires being able to study the concrete norms that constitute them as well. Those rules are tangible. Using the appropriate legal strategy, they can be found and analyzed accordingly.

---

[5] Martha Alberston Fineman. *Introduction, in* AT THE BOUNDARIES OF LAW. FEMINISM AND LEGAL THEORY xiv (M.A. Fineman & N.S. Thomadsen eds., 1991).

Therefore, this book promotes a dual approach to studying law as well. It states that studying law means more than understanding legal concepts: it also means researching the law, finding the tangible aspect of those concepts. This approach is not new to critical legal thinking. It resonates with any dialectical approach to study theory through practice, but it is especially necessary when studying American law, due to its social importance. The interconnection between the ends—legitimate order—and the means—legal activity—becomes apparent only when you have access to both the concepts and their tangible normative source. Additionally, effective American legal research is not possible absent a minimal understanding of the American legal system and of its major idiosyncrasies.

Legal systems—through their concrete legal norms—are meant to forge social legitimate order. As societies are dynamic entities, governing them is a dynamic task as well. Concrete norms by their nature, thus, have finite life. They need to change in order to accommodate a society's social and political needs, moral standards, and sense of justice. The American ideal of legitimate order has remained unchanged for a few centuries. However, when you study different areas of American law, you see that norms change continually. Thus, when researching the law you need to always update your research, but you also need to remember that those changes are limited in nature: they must conform to the core American cultural values that the "rule of law" defends. For example, on one hand, because all statutes are open to judicial review, and during that process courts may even alter or annul statutory provisions by declaring them unconstitutional, when you search for statutes you also need to search for case law. On the other hand, knowing that that change has a limited nature will make it easier for you to accept the lack of results that updating your legal research will often produce.

This book aspires to offer an intellectual point of view about American law, by laying down the foundation of life-long critical legal thinking skills. It aspires to guide you to always remember that irrespective of its abstract appearance, law has a tangible facet. How do you reach the goal of legitimate order? Why is a federal or state statutory approach favored? These are questions that will always be with you in your studies of the diverse bodies of law.

It also aspires to direct you in your legal search to the appropriate sources, which help you understand the limits of your research. How do you know the value of this individual right? Where do you search for it? Is this the appropriate source you should use? Is this the only source you should check? Is this enabling norm still good law? These are all questions that you should become familiar with during your legal research.

During your studies you will discover that sometimes it is easier to gain knowledge of American law in its abstract facet than in its concrete representation. Legal research is heavily dependant on your financial resources. For example, this book will point out to you the numerous free-of-charge repositories of law. However, it will also point out that you cannot update your search reliably unless you have access to fee-based electronic databases, such as Lexis and Westlaw. This book will make it easier for you to be aware of both the strengths and weaknesses of your legal research.

This book will briefly describe the meanings of law in American legal studies. It will also explain the sources of American public law. Thus, you will learn about the branches of the government and how they all make American law: Congress passes statutes, courts hand down decisions, the President issues Presidential orders, and administrative agencies issue regulations. You will learn about the repositories of American public law. You will learn that statutes are collected in codes, court decisions in reporters, and agency regulations in codes as well. It will become apparent that while the sources of law are accessible to the public both in paper and electronic formats, you need to choose a specific repository according to your legal research query. The information you have when you start your search will control your choices.

Thus, this book will bring you up to speed and fill in the gap between your understanding about American law and that of a native student. It will bring you to the same level of understanding of American law as any American law student. This book will help you understand all these and more about the sources of law.

Naturally, understanding American law is a long process. It takes law practitioners years of study and practice. However, like learning any other subject, when studying law one starts with the ABC's. It makes a difference how any first class is taught. If the teaching process is not right, it can discourage people from pursuing the subject any further. Hopefully this book is the right beginning of what could become a lifetime interest in American law—starting with the ways in which it works, and ending with how and whether law can be an instrument of justice, for example.[6]

However, do not browse through this book hoping to find the equivalent of a legal cook-book, a "how-to" manual. You need to have a minimal understanding of the social functions of American law, and then about how concrete legal norms work. There are ways to locate specific norms as there are ways to make sure that they are still good law. This book will provide answers to all these questions. However, there are no recipes worth following in doing legal research other than a few major principles that will be further detailed. From a theoretical point of view, it will always depend on what you know when you start your research, and what you want to have learned by the end of the process. From a practical point of view it will always depend on your time availability and finances. Researching American law reliably can be expensive at both levels: its finding component may require some time exclusively devoted to locate the law, while its updating component relies heavily on fee-based databases.

This book is structured into six chapters. Chapters 1 and 2 will talk about law and explain what it is. They will attempt to decipher the double meaning of law as an ideal of a temporal order, where the rule of law strives to make sure that the concrete temporal rules achieve. They will also provide an understanding of the limits within which concrete legal norms may change in order to help you successfully strategize your legal research.

Chapter 3 will lay down the foundation of the process of finding the law. It will emphasize the role of scholarly publications as ways of finding the specific legal rules and of understanding their

6 *Id.* at 9–12.

scope within our democracy. It will also talk about the sources of law and the governmental institutions that devise public law. It will explain where the law is while it will give you a sense of how American law emerges and works. It will briefly point out the repositories of law: those sources of law that represent the published manifestations of the law. In legal research those are called "primary sources." It will bring law closer to you as it talks about the various print and online repositories of law. It will pay distinct attention to the online repositories that can be freely accessed from any computer with Internet access. Through this chapter, it will become apparent that there are many ways to access American legal norms.

The next three chapters of the book will talk about each major source of public law in the United States. Chapter 4 will focus on statutory law. It will explain what it is, and where and how you find it. Chapter 5 will focus on decisional law. Similarly, it will explain what it is, where it is, and how you can find it. Chapter 6 will follow the same pattern while focusing on administrative law. These chapters will draw on the information presented in Chapters 1, 2, and 3 and will detail the sources for each type of law.

Chapter 1
A Dynamic Legal System Shaped by Long-Lasting Principles

> [. . .] law is a rule of civil conduct [. . .] commanding what is right and prohibiting what is wrong.
>
> *Blackstone's The Study, Nature, and Extent of the Law*

> When we study law we are not studying a mystery [. . .] The means of the study are a body of reports, of treatises, and of statutes, in this country and in England, extending back for six hundred years [. . .]
>
> *O.W. Holmes, Jr. "The Path of the Law"*
> *10 Harvard Law Review 457, 457 (1897)*

A. INTRODUCTION

It has often been remarked that the American people have an "uncanny reverence for law."[1] Lawyers breed in large numbers, and we are maybe the most litigious nation on earth. One reason may be that we are never too far from law or legal discourse. Talks about individual rights and due process of law thrive in school, at home, on TV, and even MTV. Legal concepts generate perhaps more popular culture (including songs and movies) than they do academic writings.

American general culture often covers legal knowledge. Many know that state law defines murder and manslaughter, and many know that intention tells them apart. Of course, few know what

---

1 DANIEL J. BOORSTIN, AMERICA AND THE IMAGE OF EUROPE: REFLECTIONS ON AMERICAN THOUGHT vi–vii (1960).

state law is or how to find those statutes, such as the Pennsylvania ones,[2] that define those felonies, and distinguish between intentional and involuntary homicide.

In the same way European high school students learn about Bergson, and other little known philosophers,[3] for their graduation examination—which the French call *le baccalauréat*—Americans take civics classes and learn about law. American high school graduates often know that the Supreme Court has been the guarantor of our individual freedoms, and phrases such as "You are breaking the law" and "I will take you to court" are part of the popular vocabulary.

Indeed, unlike other nations, we can say that the Supreme Court gave us the right to purchase contraception,[4] and the right to have a private sexual relationship with a same-sex partner.[5] For example, in 1965, in *Griswold v. Connecticut*, the Supreme Court recognized a zone of intimate privacy for married couples, which covered the woman's right to decide whether her marital sexual conduct was reproductive or not.[6] In 2003, in *Lawrence v. Texas*, the Court similarly recognized a zone of intimate privacy for same-sex couples.[7]

Americans also know about the impact the Secretary of the Interior's listing of a species as endangered has on the future of industrial projects within the area where that species cohabitates. Indeed, here, the snail darter put an end to a dam project, as a

---

[2] *See, e.g.*, Pennsylvania law: under Pennsylvania law 18 PA. CONS. STAT. ANN. § 2501 "A person is guilty of criminal homicide [murder in the first degree, defined in 2502(a)] if he intentionally . . . causes the death of another human being."

[3] In 1994 the French high school students were tested in Saint Augustin, Bergson, and Spinoza. *See Les annales du baccalauréat—épreuve de philosophie juin 1994, available at* http://www.adminet.com/graticiels/philo_jun-94.html.

[4] Griswold v. Connecticut, 381 U.S. 479 (1965).

[5] Lawrence v. Texas, 539 U.S. 558 (2003).

[6] Griswold v. Connecticut, 381 U.S. 479 (1965).

[7] Lawrence v. Texas, 539 U.S. 558 (2003).

result of a Supreme Court decision.[8] In 1978, in *TVA v. Hill*, the Supreme Court recognized that "the snail darter is a living entity which is genetically distinct and reproductively isolated from other fishes" according to the Endangered Species Act of 1973. It thus prohibited TVA, a federal agency, from finishing the construction of the Tellico dam on the Tennessee River, although it was virtually completed, because it would have eradicated the snail darter population.

How does this widespread legal knowledge affect you? It suffices to say that if it is not part of your legal baggage, you need to become aware of your deficiency and overcome its potential hindrance of your studies. There are a few steps that you can take to avoid it. First, you should focus on understanding basic concepts of American law so you avoid any pitfalls by making inaccurate assumptions. Of course, there are concepts that may be present in both your own and the American legal system and you need to be aware of them and of the fact that they may have different meanings. Understanding the nuances of the legal jargon will only facilitate your legal studies and help you be effective in strategizing legal research. Once you are able to identify commonalities and differences between your own legal system and the American legal system you should go one step further and identify the sources of American public law: how they make the law, where the law is located, and how you can find it. Only then you will have freed your intellectual prowess to concentrate on the specific legal subjects of American law, on their rich subtleties, and study and research them proficiently.

---

8 *See* TVA v. Hill, 437 U.S. 153 (1978) ("the Secretary [of the Interior] formally listed the snail darter as an endangered species on October 8, 1975. 40 Fed. Reg. 47,505–47,506; *see* 50 C.F.R. § 17.11(i) (1976). In so acting, it was noted that "the snail darter is a living entity which is genetically distinct and reproductively isolated from other fishes." 40 Fed. Reg. 47,505).

B. AMERICAN LAW HAS BOTH AN ABSTRACT AND A CONCRETE FACET; ONLY THE LATTER CONSTITUTES THE OBJECT OF LEGAL RESEARCH

That both "law" and "laws" are concepts with multiple meanings may not come as a surprise to you. In any legal system, law is often viewed as the means to reach an ideal of legitimate order, while laws are specific types of recorded legal norms that make that ideal possible.

Law is also a branch of knowledge that studies the rules governing people's behavior in relation to each other.[9] Law is both discourse about power and power in action. The discourse studies legal rules[10] from a multitude of perspectives. If legal philosophy, in its wider sense promotes "general reflection on the nature of legal institutions,"[11] legal methods and legal research explain how those institutions (the legislative, executive, and administrative branches) work and how we can research their products (statutes, cases, and administrative rules, regulations, or decisions).

Thus, if law, including American law, aims[12] at "making society more stable and enabling people to flourish,"[13] then in legal philosophy you study how that goal is reached—the end of the process—and in legal research you learn how to locate the means to reach that end—the concrete norms of conduct that the state enforces when they are violated. For example, society maintains order by enforcing particular rules. If you do not pay your rent, the landlord can evict you, and if you refuse to leave the premises, the sheriff—or another law enforcement officer—will forcibly move you and your belongings out into the street. Those rules can easily become the object of legal research.

---

9 JOHN CORBIN, FIND THE LAW IN THE LIBRARY. A GUIDE TO LEGAL RESEARCH (1989).

10 *Id.*

11 MORRIS R. COHEN, AMERICAN THOUGHT: A CRITICAL SKETCH 135 (1954).

12 TONY HONORÉ, ABOUT LAW. AN INTRODUCTION 1 et seq. (2000).

13 *Id.* at 1.

Some of those concrete rules are known under the term "laws." They are man-made because they are passed by citizens organized in assemblies and thus different from the laws of nature that one studies in physics, biology, or chemistry classes. As often observed, unlike the laws of nature or society, which describe natural or social phenomena, legal norms prescribe our conduct and make our future predictable. For example, legal norms divide our actions in lawful and unlawful. Legal norms also identify which unlawful actions are criminal, and which ones are punished with loss of liberty, or even with loss of life. To the extent that the severity of the punishment is rationalized as a necessary social deterrent of that activity, legal sanctions create legal obedience, and a predictable tomorrow.

In all legal systems the abstract and the concrete aspect of the law are interconnected. The degree varies from system to system. Generally, if you think about constitutional rights and principles, within the frame of the American legal system, you will first tend to define them abstractly. But rights do not exist abstractly. They can be found only in "historical constitutions and political systems."[14] Furthermore, such rights are interpreted and "actualized"[15] in the context of a given society and its legal order. The right to own property has very specific meanings from one historic period to another and from one social class to another.[16]

Moreover, like all domestic legal norms, American legal norms also are expected to make the ideal of legitimate social order feasible. As W. Friedmann remarked, every legal system is supposed to implement a just legal order whose meaning, of course, changes from one historical epoch to another and from one society to another.[17]

---

14 JURGEN HABERMAS, BETWEEN FACTS AND NORMS. CONTRIBUTIONS TO A DISCOURSE THEORY OF LAW AND DEMOCRACY 194 (1996).

15 *Id.*

16 On the rights of the American lower class, also known as the "underclass," *see, e.g.*, CHRISTOPHER JENCKS, RETHINKING SOCIAL POLICY. RACE, POVERTY, AND THE UNDERCLASS (1992).

17 W. FRIEDMANN, LEGAL THEORY 21 et seq. (5th ed. 1967).

Norms achieve Friedmann's "purposeful enterprise"[18] by remaining open to change: they mirror all changes societies, which are living bodies, encounter: changes in people's needs as well as changes in their mores and in their perception of social ideals. Thus, while the ideal of legitimate order remains constant, its meaning changes in time. What constitutes legitimate today is different from its 19th century meaning, and, as shown below, what was legitimate in the 18th century lost that status in the 19th century.

For all these reasons, in this book, law is approached as a concept, a signifier, with two meanings. Law signifies both the ideal of order and predictability in any given society and the concrete legal norms that make it feasible.

The American ideal of order is often perceived under the guise of the role of the "rule of law." Perhaps it is easier to explain how legal norms help achieve this ideal if we explain the role played by the "rule of law." Technically the "rule of law" can be regarded as a principle of sovereignty of the laws over men. Many of you must have heard the famous but cryptic phrase describing the aspirations of the American Founding Fathers to create "a government of laws and not of men."[19] More simply, the American ideal of government requires a legal system that reduces the impact of human whims in the government to a minimum.

Think about the rule of law as a fundamental political ideal for the Anglo-American notion of good government, as the intermediary between the concrete legal norm and the ideal of order that norm is supposed to achieve. The rule of law is supposed to shape the American legal system according to the political ideals of social stability and predictability.

While the rule of law is a controversial political ideal, and its requirements are not set in stone, they can be nevertheless summarized. For example, Michael Moore identified six values of the rule of law—separation of powers, equality and formal justice, lib-

---

18 *Id.* at 21.

19 Constitution of Massachusetts: Declaration of Rights, art. 30 (1780).

erty and notice, substantive fairness, procedural fairness, and efficient administration[20]—and F. A. Hayek, more conservatively,[21] identified only two main requisites—generality and predictability.[22]

The rule of law is a debatable concept. However, few deny its role as a legal watchdog. Thus, if we concentrate on its function, its requirements can be viewed as being procedural and substantive. The procedural requirements impose restraints in the way government exercises its legal authority, and the substantive requirements impose constraints on the content of the exercised legal authority, so that they do not violate a vital core of American cultural values, which translate into the American ideal of legitimate order and predictability. Those values are, of course, vastly inspired by the British ones, due to the historical development of the American society—a former British colony.

When a body of concrete rules becomes perceived by the majority as illegitimate, the system replaces them, because one of the constraints the "rule of law" imposes on the American legal system is preserving legitimate order. Of course, there are many problems with the concept of legitimate order. Nevertheless, its very existence emphasizes what is commendable about the American legal system. Its purpose is to minimize individual whims and create a social order accepted by the many and not imposed by the few.

The requirements imposed by the rule of law affect the concrete norms to the extent that those, which do not comply, are "rejected." Additionally, as mentioned before, legal norms govern human behavior, which is open to constant change. Within the U.S. legal system, legal norms exist only to the extent they ensure the American ideal of social order and stability. This ideal mirrors the socio-political needs of each historical period, as well as its

---

20 Michael Moore, *A Natural Law Theory of Interpretation*, 58 S. CAL. L. REV. 277 (1985).

21 Steven J. Burton. *Particularism, Discretion, and the Rule of Law*, 36 NOMOS 178, 180 (1994).

22 F.A. HAYEK, THE ROAD TO SERFDOM (1944).

sense of justice and moral standards. Concrete norms, which cannot play that role, are changed, amended, or replaced with others more suited to promote the society's ideal of stability.

The next example is sufficiently dramatic to exemplify the interplay between the abstract and concrete facet of American law. It will illustrate the nature of the dynamism of this legal system. It will show how the rule of law acts as a constraint on the American legal system to dispose of those norms whose content ceases to promote a legitimate order according to core Anglo-American values.

This complex nature of the American legal system should translate into your constant need to update your legal research to make sure that your concrete findings are still part of the legal system, in other words, are still good law. Additionally, if you understand that all changes must come within a well-defined cultural frame you will freely accept the often lack of or the meek results of your updating efforts.

C. INDIVIDUAL NORMS ARE OPEN TO CHANGE

The rule of law has been identified with the values promoted by Western democracies, and especially with the Anglo-American ones. Within these cultural limits, the rule of law promotes social stability.

Understanding how the rule of law works is understanding the core Anglo-American values as well. For example, the American and English cultures and values remained similar even after the American colonies gained their independence from the British Empire. They are rooted in liberal individualism.

Liberal individualism has both a religious and a secular component. Its religious facet has been explained as relying on the Protestant Reformation's emphasis on faith and individual contact with God, instead of a mediated-by-Church divine contact. Its secular element relies on modern secular philosophy, which focuses on the needs of the individual instead of those of the community. Moreover, it is ingrained in the classical *laissez-faire* economics of unrestrained competition;[23] it does not value communitarian approaches to life, and thus it mostly relies on individual rights against the government.

As a result of these common ideals, American and English political institutions have remained similar even after the American colonies gained their independence. There is one notable exception, however. America lacks the lawmaking institution of the monarchy.

The two legal regimes differ also. For example, England's legal system does not have a judicial institution at its pinnacle. Nevertheless, the American legal system continued its British "common law" tradition. Both systems have come to rely on judge-made law (court decisions) as a better-suited means to promote their cultural values, rather than on assembly-made law (statutory law), which traditionally defines the "civil law" system—the other major Western legal system. A common law approach to law, unlike the civil law one, emphasizes gradual, almost individualistic, legal change. By its very own nature, judge-made law relies on solving the conflict of the interested parties that brought the specific lawsuit; each court decision is binding upon the parties to the lawsuit. Of course, due to the precedential value of court decisions in common law systems, a court decision from a superior court is expected to dictate the ways in which similar factual cases are decided by inferior courts. Still, absent a new decision, the subsequent parties are not bound directly by the precedent. Unlike judge-made law, whose effect is incremental by nature because it binds only the few parties to the litigation, a statute is binding upon large populations from the moment of its enactment.

This similarity survived at least one major institutional difference. For example, until late into the 19th century, almost a century after the American colonies liberated themselves from the English yoke, there were American states, such as Delaware and Kentucky,[24] which held human beings as property. At the state

23 MORRIS R. COHEN, THE FAITH OF A LIBERAL, at 59 et seq. (1946).

24 *Id.* at 281.

level, American law contained complex property rules, which held the slave as the "absolute property of his owner."[25] At the federal level the institution of slavery was used to allot more Congressional representation to the states that recognized it. Article I, Section 2, paragraph 3 of the Constitution implicitly sanctioned the institution—although never by name—when it counted slaves as three-fifths taxable citizens.[26] Thus, a state that recognized slavery had more representatives in Congress than a state that had the same number of voters but no slaves.

On the other hand, the English legal system never recognized the institution of slavery. In fact, "A slave or negro, the instant he lands in England, becomes a freeman; that is, the law will protect him in his enjoyment of his person, and his property," Blackstone wrote in 1765.[27]

Eventually the American legal system abolished this institution. It is worth mentioning that the change did not affect the existing principles of liberal individualism, which persisted. Notwithstanding slavery, the American and the English societies and their legal systems remained similar. How do we explain the similarity and its stability?

First it should be noted that to the extent slavery was part of the American property rules, it had a limited role in promoting social stability and predictability, according to the contemporary social values. To the extent that slavery was a body of legal norms, like all such norms it was open to change according to both the social and political context surrounding that human behavior and the views that the majority held about it.

When slavery ceased to correspond to the American ideal of legitimate order, as viewed by the majority, it stopped promoting social stability within the core of contemporary social values. When

---

25 ROBERT SHAW, A LEGAL HISTORY OF SLAVERY 157 (1991).

26 6 ENCYCLOPEDIA OF AMERICAN CONSTITUTION Appendix 3, at 2957 (2d ed.).

27 EHRLICH'S BLACKSTONE, at v and 71 (1959).

the majority decided that slavery needed to be abandoned, America faced a bloody civil war. Indeed, despite President Lincoln's insistence that the Civil War was only "a struggle against secession"[28] and not one to end the institution of slavery, the war had the effect of constraining the confederate states to accept constitutional amendments that made slavery illegal.

The 13th Amendment "upgraded" the American legal system: it outlawed slavery. As a result, it mirrored the contemporary moral standards. On December 18, 1865, the 13th Amendment's ban on slavery and involuntary servitude within "any place subject to [the United States] jurisdiction" became effective.[29] Thus, ridding itself of unjust laws, the system promoted order and stability.[30] As a result, circumscribed in legal normativism, slavery, as an institution, was dissolved within the legal system.

This change in the American legal system can be explained as the result of the requirements imposed by the rule of law. The rule of law requires that all legal norms correspond to certain procedural and substantive constraints. Otherwise, they cannot promote social order and stability within the chosen type of democratic government. When legal norms lose their aura of legitimacy, they are replaced according to well-established procedures. Similarly, when legal norms are the result of legitimate exercise of power, and their content does not violate the core social values that define the social ideal of order, despite their arguable merit, those rules are not replaced.

The next three examples will further illustrate the dynamic nature of the American legal system within the well-established political limits of the rule of law. Although apparently at random, legal norms are changed only when the institutions in charge of overseeing the functioning of the legal system perceive it necessary. Statutes are declared unconstitutional only when aggrieved

---

28 ROBERT SHAW, A LEGAL HISTORY OF SLAVERY 279 (1991).

29 *Id.* at 282.

30 Ian Shapiro, *Introduction, in* NOMOS, at 1 (1994).

parties raise that issue and courts find the argument persuasive. Court decisions are superseded by statutes or overruled by other court decisions also when they do not fit within the legal values promoted by the American legal system. Administrative rules and decisions are open to change by the issuing administrative body, statutes, or courts.

The next examples will illustrate a few of the contemporary idiosyncrasies of the American legal system that you should be aware of in you legal studies. Legal norms are open to change, but change comes within cumbersome procedures. Often social and legal change depends on the existence of an aggrieved party willing to start the process. However, unlike in a civil law system, where researching includes updating by the very nature of the system—the codified statute will mention its most recent amendment—in a common law system, such as the American one, researching does not include updating. Statutes are open to change that comes from courts. Sometimes the codified version of federal statutes will include the most recent court opinion that bears on that statute. But there is no foolproof assurance about that. Moreover, statutes are collected in separate repositories from court opinions. Aside from these mechanical aspects of legal research, you need to develop a "feeling" for it that rests on a clear understanding of how the systems works.

D. LEGAL NORMS ARE OPEN TO JUDICIAL AND CONGRESSIONAL SCRUTINY

The United States is a federation of 50 states. Its governing body combines a centralized federal body and 50 state governments. At both levels, each branch of the government makes law that conforms to the requirement of the rule of law. They are both procedural and substantive restraints.

The rule of law requires any legal system to be stable. Only stable systems can aspire to satisfy the requirements of generality and prospectivity. So, once an assembly has properly enacted a statute, absent an aggrieved party, there is no judiciary recourse, and absent judiciary process, it often makes more political sense to leave it untouched. The sign of a good government is the diversity of its norms that cover as many political interests as possible. Norms that may not necessarily achieve any regulatory effect, and thus may not be an example of legal normativism, may, nevertheless, represent specific interests uncovered by other statutes. Through such norms, the legal system is able to represent a large constituency, which is needed in any representative democracy. Again, they will rarely be changed.

The next examples should also introduce you to another important aspect of the American legal heritage: the interplay between the legislative and the judicial branches. For more than a century, the judiciary has been at the pinnacle of the American legal system deciding what the Constitution is and what rules violate the Constitution. The American judiciary is in charge of interpreting the law enacted by the legislative branch, and sometimes courts—minorities—have overruled statutes that mirror majoritarian positions. Thus, you always need to make sure that your legal research covers court decisions.

The examples below illustrate that to the extent each lawmaking governmental branch respects procedural restraints and exercises publicly justifiable power, the norms they make will rarely be questioned or changed, irrespective of their social merit as long as their content does not defy the values promoted by the rule of law. When you study American law, this observation will help you understand why some Supreme Court decisions are still good law or why others are being incrementally changed. When you do legal research, the above observation will help you remember that while you constantly need to update your results often, there is nothing out there affecting your research results.

The next three examples will hopefully make it easier for you to see the interplay between legal stability and change, which is only another facet of the interplay between the abstract and concrete facet of American law. They should both emphasize the need for updating and the difficulty of ending your research when you may not find anything new to add. Sometimes, you feel that there should be something more and there is not. Developing a sense of confidence in your research results is also part of the complexities of American legal research. When you become aware of these idiosyncrasies of the American legal system you will also understand how to better strategize your legal research.

1. Judicial and Congressional Review of Statutory Rules

When Congress passes a statute following the usual congressional procedure, and it thus exercises publicly justifiable power, we accept the rule contained in that statute as being law, or, in the words of the renowned legal philosopher Hart, we recognize it as valid, as legitimate, and we obey it. Few inquire into the merits of a piece of legislation and even fewer challenge it, even though its merits may be arguable, as long as it does not violate any constraints imposed by the "rule of law." Nevertheless, a thorough researcher will update his statutory results with a search for all relevant court decisions.

For example, in an effort to change the culture of alcohol consumption on college campuses, in December 1997, in the U.S. House of Representatives, Representative Joseph P. Kennedy II proposed a resolution aimed at changing the campus culture and at supporting healthier student choices about alcohol. That was the "Collegiate Initiative to Reduce Binge Drinking,"[31] House Resolution 321, and it called on all college and university administrators to adopt a code of principles designed to create a campus environment that deemphasizes the role of heavy drinking in student life.

Initially, the resolution was advertised as not creating "a legally binding requirement for college campuses, and as not requiring any formal voting."[32] However, soon afterwards a Senate resolu-

---

31 H.R. Res. 321, 105th Cong. (1997).

32 Alcohol Policies Project, *at* http://www.cspinet.org/booze/janalert.htm.

tion was introduced,[33] and a legislative measure followed suit. Within a year since its introduction, Congress passed the "Collegiate Initiative To Reduce Binge Drinking and Illegal Alcohol Consumption" as a binding statute.[34] No one challenged the act in court. A lot of good-will press coverage ensued.

The students' response to the legislative proposal was quick and swift. It criticized Congress's attempt to change college culture through legislation, when all it did was to outline ways to fight binge drinking in its manifestations, while it failed to address its societal or cultural causes.[35] It identified the national high drinking age as being the culprit.[36]

Some may say that there is no way to enforce that piece of legislation, and there is no clear data to gauge whether it had any real effect in making students stop heavy drinking—defined according to the 1997 study published by Harvard's School of Public Health[37]

The Resolution notes that: many college presidents rank alcohol abuse as the number one problem on campus; alcohol is a factor in the three leading causes of death for 15–24 year olds; alcohol is involved in a large percentage of campus rapes, violent crimes, student suicides, and fraternity "hazing" injuries; almost half (44 percent) of all students qualify as binge drinkers; and heavy drinking causes problems for students who drink and has "second hand" effects for other students.

33 S. Res. 192, 105th Cong. (1998). *Expressing the Sense of the Senate to Change the Culture of Alcohol Consumption on College Campuses, available at* http://thomas.loc.gov/cgi-bin/query/z?r105:S05MR8-691.

34 Higher Education Assistance Act, 20 U.S.C.A. §§ 1011h, 1011I (2000), superseding Drug-Free Schools and Communities Act of 1989, 20 U.S.C.A. §§ 1145g, 3224a. Pub. L. No. 89–329, tit. I, § 119, *added by* Pub. L. No. 105–244, tit. I, § 101(a), 112 Stat. 1596 (Oct. 7, 1998).

35 Matthew Blumenstein, *Binge drinking can't be curbed by politics* STANFORD DAILY ONLINE (Feb. 13, 1998), *at* http://www.stanforddaily.com/tempo?page=content&id=4444&repository=0001_article.

36 *Id.*

37 Henry Wechsler et al., *College Binge Drinking in the 1990s: A Continuing Problem Results of the Harvard School of Public Health 1999 College Alcohol Study, at* http://www.hsph.harvard.edu/cas/rpt2000/CAS2000rpt.shtml.

as "the consumption of at least five drinks in a row for men or four drinks in a row for women." No one can measure whether the change in the drinking behavior, if any, was a direct result of a toothless statute, which only called upon universities to appoint a task force made up of administrators, faculty, students, and greek system representatives to work toward reducing alcohol problems on campuses.

Perhaps, the norm needed to have required universities to take anti-drinking measures and to have attached financial implications to those requirements instead of encouraging universities to take steps in that direction. Nevertheless, the legislation encountered only slight initial opposition. Congress passed it as a sign that the existing culture of a well-identified segment of the population needed to be changed. It may be inept, but there is no requirement under the "rule of law" that all American legal norms be efficient. Furthermore, this law promotes drinking responsibly, which is part of the American Protestant values, and the culture promoted by the rule of law.

That being said, finding this piece of statutory law will not end your research. Due to the role played by the judiciary in American law, you will always need to make sure that there is no court decision interpreting that statute, which may adversely affect the result of your research. At the same time, there are instances when updating your research will not produce any additional documents. You need to become comfortable with that result despite your own feelings about the merits of a particular piece of legislation.

2. Judicial and Congressional Review of Court Decisions

Courts are the ultimate arbiter of justice in American law. As a result, when you research statutory or administrative law you need to check how the courts have interpreted it. Additionally, when you research case law, you need to check more recent decisions from the appropriate superior courts, or the courts of last resort from each jurisdiction as well. As shown later in this book, the federal government has a federal judiciary branch and each state government has its own state judiciary, and case law from the courts of each jurisdiction may be reversed and remanded by the court of last resort from that jurisdiction.

The U.S. Supreme Court is the ultimate legal arbiter. Its decisions, which follow the Court's well-established procedure, are seldom overruled by the Court or questioned by Congress in subsequent legislation. To the extent the content of its decisions corresponds to our contemporary values, and the Court exercises publicly justifiable power, the rule of law does not require them to be discarded, although they may be, arguably, a wrong statutory interpretation. Nevertheless, sometimes the Court decides not to follow its own precedents and reverses itself, or a congressional statute may supersede a Court's decision and render it inapplicable. As a result, while apparently rarely necessary, you still need to update and check the status of your research of Supreme Court decisions.

For example, in 1990, Congress passed the "Gun-Free School Zones Act of 1990,"[38] which declared it unlawful for any individual to posses a firearm in a school zone. Congress limited the offense to the type of firearm. In Section 922q(2)(A) Congress stated that:

> It shall be unlawful for any individual knowingly to possess a firearm *that has moved in or that otherwise affects interstate or foreign commerce* at a place that the individual knows, or has reasonable cause to believe, is a school zone.[39] (emphasis added)

Alfonso Lopez Jr., a 12th-grade student, who went to Edison High School in San Antonio, Texas, carrying a concealed .38-caliber handgun and five bullets, was charged with violating the statute. He challenged the federal statute's constitutionality, and filed a lawsuit in the appropriate federal court. The Supreme

38 18 U.S.C.A. § 922.

39 18 U.S.C.A. § 922(q)(2)(A).

Court accepted a review of the decision, by granting a writ of *certiorari*, and held that Congress did not have the authority to make firearms' possession a federal offense. In deciding the case—whose title became *United States v. Lopez*,[40] after the name of the parties involved—the Supreme Court ignored the provision underlined above and held that:

> The Act neither regulates a commercial activity nor *contains a requirement that the possession be connected in any way to interstate commerce.* We hold that the Act exceeds the authority of Congress "[t]o regulate Commerce . . . among the several States." (emphasis added)

The Supreme Court did not see any specific commercial qualification on the type of firearm involved, although it may reasonably be argued to the contrary. Its decision has remained unchallenged in Congress. While a bill to reauthorize the ban on undetectable firearms was introduced in the House last year,[41] the statutory provisions of the Gun-Free School Zones Act of 1990 continue to remain unconstitutional and thus not binding.

When the Supreme Court decides the unconstitutionality of a statute, the only recourse is for Congress to address that finding by passing another statute that incorporates the Court's suggestion. For example, in 1996, Congress passed the Communications Decency Act (CDA),[42] which criminalized using any computer network to display "indecent" material unless the content provider uses an "effective" method to restrict access to that material by anyone under the age of 18. The Supreme Court, in *Reno v. American Civil Liberties Union*, declared the statute unconstitutional.[43] In

---

40 514 U.S. 549 (1995).

41 H.R. 3348 (2004).

42 Pub. L. No. 104-104, 110 Stat. 133 (codified as amended at 47 U.S.C. § 223 (Supp. II 1996)).

43 Reno v. ACLU, 521 U.S. 844, 859–60 (1997).

1998, Congress passed the Child Online Protection Act (COPA)[44] as a follow-up to the Supreme Court's invalidation of CDA. COPA, unlike CDA, targeted only commercial Web sites and only indecent material that was "harmful to minors."[45] Nevertheless, in *Ashcroft v. American Civil Liberties Union* (2002), the Supreme Court did not give its stamp of approval to the revamped legislative version, and enjoined the state from enforcing it while it remanded the case for further examination by the lower court.[46] When the lower court's opinion reached the Supreme Court in *Ashcroft v. American Civil Liberties Union* (2004),[47] the Court held that "the statute likely violates the First Amendment"[48] and, again, refused to enforce it. But the CDA/COPA example does not reflect the average situation. Usually Congress accepts the Supreme Court's interpretations of its statutes.

Due to the position of the Supreme Court at the pinnacle of the American federal legal system, no legal research is ever finished without a comprehensive search for a Supreme Court decision on point. Of course, often such a decision does not exist. Nevertheless, your research needs to include this part of the process as well.

3. Judicial Review of Administrative Decisions

This final example will briefly focus on the interplay between administrative and decisional law. It will illustrate that administrative rules and decisions, which conform to the requirements of the rule of law and the society's ideal of stability, although open to judicial review, are rarely reversed. However, the need for updating remains, as it remains the need to develop a sense of confidence in your research results when you do not find anything

---

44 47 U.S.C. § 231(a)(1) (2000).

45 47 U.S.C. § 231(e)(6) (2000).

46 Ashcroft v. ACLU, 535 U.S. 564, 585 (2002).

47 124 S. Ct. 2783 (2004).

48 *Id.*

more. This time we will look at the product of administrative lawmaking: an agency decision.

For example, the Federal Communications Commission (FCC), upon a complaint from a father that his son heard an offensive monologue broadcast by a radio station, decided in its memorandum opinion that the "Filthy Words" monologue by comedian George Carlin contained words that depicted sexual and excretory activities. Therefore, it condemned it as indecent, according to an applicable statutory provision.[49]

Arguably, the FCC decision can be described as illegal censorship, and the federal court of appeal that reviewed it reversed it on those grounds.[50] The Supreme Court granted the writ of *certiorari* and agreed to review the decision. The Supreme Court reversed the lower court's decision and upheld the FCC's ban. In its decision, abbreviated as *FCC v. Pacifica Foundation*,[51] the Supreme Court held that:

> The FCC was warranted in concluding that indecent language within the meaning of § 1464 was used in the challenged broadcast. The words "obscene, indecent, or profane" are in the disjunctive, implying that each has a separate meaning. *Though prurient appeal is an element of "obscene," it is not an element of "indecent," which merely refers to noncomformance with accepted standards of morality.*[52] (emphasis added)

The Court let us see its reasoning: it upholds administrative decisions that do not offend the core American values, and it will reverse the ones that violate them. Those values are rooted in morality, justice, and liberal individualism. It is the role of the rule

49 18 U.S.C.A. § 1464.

50 FCC v. Pacifica Found., 556 F.2d 9 (1977).

51 FCC v. Pacifica Found., 438 U.S. 726 (1978).

52 *Id.* at 727.

of law to preserve a legal system that promotes those values. It is not the role of the rule of law to advance a perfect legal system.

However, to the extent that such a principle works, concrete norms are open to various types of change according to the demands of the rule of law that requires all legal norms to promote legitimate order of an ever-changing social body. This potential change and the hierarchical structure rooted in the common law features of the American legal system demand that you update all your research endeavors and make sure that your search has covered appropriate court decisions as well.

E. THE ABSTRACT FACET OF AMERICAN LAW IS SIMILAR TO THAT OF ANY DOMESTIC LEGAL SYSTEM

Studying and researching law are heavily influenced by the basic characteristics of each legal system and by the extent you master them. If you remember that there are many common elements among all domestic legal systems, you may be able to focus on the idiosyncrasies of the American legal system faster and achieve better results in your legal studies. First of all, all domestic legal systems have an abstract and a concrete facet. They all promote social order through concrete norms.

For example, the discourse about the "rule of law" belongs to the historical discourse about the constraints all legal systems face. However, the constraints exercised by the rule of law are emphatically secular, and they are of relatively recent origin.

The rule of law functions as a constraint on the American legal system. Perhaps its functions are not familiar to you. But you already know that all legal systems have known various societal constraints that made possible the preservation of every given type of state-based social organization. For example, the Soviet legal system was shaped by constraints, which one may regard as similar in nature to those imposed by the rule of law. Due to them, the legal system contained only norms that mirrored the Soviet societal values. For example, Soviet law did not allow private ownership of the means of production, such as an enterprise.[53] To the contrary, American law does not recognize the Soviet-type of property, and the only property norms that it contains are those focused on private property. The difference in their property laws underscores the difference between the social values the two societies herald as fundamental.

Such basic understanding of how all-legal systems work will let you form appropriate expectations in your legal studies. Especially if you research law using non-authoritative sources available through the Internet, understanding this basic principle will assist your research and signal that you should discard those results that do not fit within the American society's general values, for example. Thus, think about the rule of law as the intellectual reminder of your need to update your research. If courts are the ultimate arbiter of what violates the requirements imposed by the "rule of law," then you always need to know how the courts have interpreted any statutory or administrative law.

As mentioned above, legal systems have always faced constraints.[54] Whether they are summoned under the "rule of law" or studied separately as legitimacy, morality, and justice, they are known to you to a large extent.

People freely obey those concrete norms if they view them as legitimate, moral, and just. The American rule of law is aware of these demands imposed on legal systems and incorporates those values within its substantive requirements.

A brief review of these constraints will further make the similarities between the American legal system and your own legal sys-

---

53 For a generally accepted analysis of the cultural differences between a socialist and capitalist society, *see, e.g.*, F.A. HAYEK, THE ROAD TO SERFDOM 32 et seq. (1944).

54 For an explanatory debate about the limitations on government in the Middle Ages and the legal limits of the "Prince," be them even those of the will of God, *see, e.g.*, Brian Tierney, *"The Prince Is Not Bound by the Laws." Acursius and the Origins of the Modern State*, 5 COMP. STUD. IN SOC'Y & HISTORY 378, 379, 388, and 389 (1963).

tem more transparent. At the same time, the rich and multifaceted nature of the American legal system will become more obvious and, with it, the idiosyncrasies that spring from it. Among those is a comparatively complex research and updating process.

First we will briefly focus on legitimacy. There are many ways to define legitimacy. For example, it has been explained through the source of legal norms: God, nature (the natural order of things), or the state of people. The Christian natural law tradition was based on the obvious superiority of God as the legitimizing source of law. The civic republican natural law tradition emphasized the state of nature as the ultimate legitimizing source of law, while the positivist tradition emphasized the state—the political human institution—as the ultimate source of legitimacy.

The classic legal theories that focus on legitimacy are natural and positive law theories.[55] All natural law theories legitimize a legal system through divine or natural power. At their core is that idea that legal principles simply exist as they manifest themselves to the universal conscience of mankind. Of course, they all acknowledge differences among domestic legal systems (human laws), but those are explained as due to differences in legal cultures, or using Hegel's expression, to the ways humans mediate the divine principles of law.[56] Of course, there are many variations within this classical school of thought.

Positive law theories focus on legitimacy also. They emphasize the state (historically, the city-state[57]) as the ultimate source of law.

---

55 This does not mean that there are no other theories focused on this issue, including sociological theories of law, utilitarianism, etc.

56 G.W.F. HEGEL, PHENOMENOLOGY OF SPIRIT 287 (A.V. Miller trans., 1977) (Human law in its universal existence is the community, in its activity in general is the manhood of the community, in its real and effective activity is the government). *See also* SIMONE GOYARD-FABRE, LES FONDEMENTS DE L'ORDRE JURIDIQUE, at 37 (1992).

57 RICHARD W. MANSBACH & YALE H. FERGUSON, POLITIES: AUTHORITY, IDENTITIES, AND CHANGE (1996).

"La loi, [wrote Carré de Malberg] est le fait étatique positif."[58] Law is the existing positive law.

The American legal thought has also dealt with legitimacy issues from both a natural and positive law perspective. For example, Thomas Jefferson justified the American Revolution on the illegitimate nature of British law, which had violated unalienable rights of the people.[59] Later, in the 18th century, James Wilson further explained the legitimacy of the American legal system as residing in God and the will of the people. Unlike monarchist theories, which legitimized legal norms through the divine connection between the king and God, American legal thought always thrived on the principle of legitimacy derived from the sovereign people. For example, James Wilson insisted that:

> The supreme power or sovereign power of the society resided in the citizens at large; and that, therefore, they always retain the right of abolishing, altering or amending their constitution, at whatever time, and in whatever manner, they shall deem it expedient.[60]

American legal thought continued the major progress added by English legal theories. Both the natural and positivist English legal thought viewed the man-made laws more than mere commands from God translated by men into laws. It viewed legal norms as rooted in the social compact made between the government and its sovereign people.

Briefly, the American natural legal thought was originally mostly built on Locke's social contract, and not on the classical and Christian explanation of the origin of the state.[61] Although a nat-

---

58 Cities—Polis, are the oldest forms of political organizations. SIMONE GOYARD-FABRE, LES FONDEMENTS DE L'ORDRE JURIDIQUE, at 99 (1992) (internal quotes omitted).

59 DAVID RICHARDS, FOUNDATIONS OF AMERICAN CONSTITUTIONALISM 18–30 (1989).

60 1 THE WORKS OF JAMES WILSON 17 (1804).

61 Discussing the American natural law theorists that followed the

ural law theorist, Locke's social contract was limited: Its players—the sovereign people and the government—had limited powers. The sovereign people gave up certain rights so that the government could be able to function within restricted boundaries. As a result, the U.S. Constitution forged a limited federal government. Under the guise of "federalism" the sovereign people delimited federal government power.

> We the People of the United States, in Order to form a more perfect Union, establish Justice, insure domestic Tranquility, provide for the common defence, promote the general Welfare, and secure the Blessings of Liberty to ourselves and our Posterity, do ordain and establish this Constitution for the United States of America.

The people preserved their inalienable or natural rights. The constitutionally recognized fundamental rights were the right to life, liberty, and property.

This combination of inborn right to individual liberty and vested property has characterized the role of the rule of law within the American legal system from its revolutionary beginnings. In fact, the American Revolution can be viewed as a response to an illegitimate act of the legislatures to restrain such a fundamental act. The Stamp Act can be viewed as a non-legitimate property law statute that attempted to take property from the Americans—by taxing them—and give it to the English. Morris Cohen noted last century, a direct nexus between the American Revolution and the American legislatures' impotence in regulating property rights. It took them a long time to be able to legitimately pass statutes that restrained those fundamental rights.[62]

Briefly, the American positivism comes through Hobbes. It is worth noting that Hobbes viewed the law as the command of the monarch and thus its primary source was the collection of king's

---

Christian explanation of the origin of state, *see* James McClellan, *Joseph Story's Natural Law Philosophy*, 5 BENCHMARK 85 (1994).

62 MORRIS R. COHEN, AMERICAN THOUGHT. A CRITICAL SKETCH 142 (1954).

statutes, and not judicial opinions.[63] Although debatable in the 17th century[64] Britain, today, indeed, statutes seem to prevail as the primary source of law in the American legal system, despite its strong common law features.

Both natural and positive law theories continued to be developed in the Anglo-American legal tradition, as questions about the reasons beyond our obedience of the legal rule only increased in our days. (See Fig. 3.) Lon Fuller, for example, talked about the interplay between the need for a legitimate source of law: the sovereign law-making authority, which itself is determined by law, and the law itself.[65] From a natural law perspective, Fuller focused on law as a particular means to an end, an enterprise of governing human conduct, and on the "internal morality" of the law.[66] He viewed the latter the reason for legal obedience. At the opposite theoretical end, H.L.A. Hart in *The Concept of Law*,[67] for example, propels the discussion about law to legal validity,[68] which offered additional explanations for legal obedience.[69] Hart's explanation starts with Max Weber's observation about coercion (avenging the norm's violation[70]) and goes further connecting the traditional legal value of justice (the result of appraisal) to non-law values such as fairness.

---

63 DIALOGUE BETWEEN A PHILOSOPHER AND A STUDENT OF THE COMMON LAWS OF ENGLAND 53 (1994).

64 J.H. Hexter, *Thomas Hobbes and the Law*, 65 CORNELL L. REV. 471, 471–478 (1979–80).

65 *See, e.g.*, LON FULLER, THE PROBLEMS OF JURISPRUDENCE (1949).

66 LON FULLER, THE MORALITY OF LAW (1964).

67 H.L.A. HART, THE CONCEPT OF LAW (2d ed. 1997).

68 *Id.* at 100–10.

69 For a concise but enlightening discussion regarding the "Hart-Fuller Debate" that materialized in the *Harvard Law Review* (1958), *see* Brian Bix., *Natural Law Theory*, 8, 13–15, *in* PHILOSOPHY OF LAW (Joel Feinberg & Jules Coleman eds., 7th ed. 2004).

70 MAX WEBER, LAW IN ECONOMY AND SOCIETY (Max Rheinstein ed., 1954).

Fig. 3
The U.S. Constitution and Natural Rights

On its Web site created to help new citizens pass the Civics Exam, the U.S. government reaffirms the constitutional guarantee of natural rights, labeled as "INHERENT RIGHTS," to both citizens and non-citizens who live in the United States.

> "The principle of inherent rights was first written in the Declaration of Independence. The Founding Fathers believed that the right to *life, liberty and the pursuit of happiness* was very important.
>
> This right is the basis for all of the rights listed in the Constitution and its amendments.
> These include:
>
> - right to freedom of religion;
> - right to freedom of speech;
> - right to bear arms, or to own weapons (a special permit is required);
> - right to a trial when accused of a crime, and to know of what crime one is accused; and,
> - right to own property and to expect the government to help protect private property."
>
> http://uscis.gov/graphics/services/natz/usstruct.pdf.

Rooted in positivism is the main American school of legal thought: realism, and its late 20th-century heir, critical legal studies (CLS). Both see law as a state product, except for the private rules such as those used in the common law tradition of contractual free bargaining, for example.[71] However, as Oliver Wendell Holmes, Jr., Karl Llewellyn, or John Dewey pointed out, American realism is less interested in issues of legitimacy of the source of law as the reason for our legal obedience than in studying the social role of the law. American realism is about what the law "is" instead

---

[71] Duncan Kennedy, *Form and Substance in Private Law Adjudication*, 89 HARV. L. REV. 1685, 1763 (1975–76).

of what the law "ought" to be. The greatest achievement of the realists was the emphasis on the fact that law was a means to social objectives and law needs to be measured by its social consequences.

Legitimacy, thus, can be related to the sources of public law and the ways those sources exercise their authority. Understanding the discourse of natural and positive rights in American law allows you to be more flexible and search for statutory, decisional, or administrative law to support your argument. Furthermore, when there is nothing authoritative on point, as the Supreme Court has stated, then, any persuasive source is useful within certain limits. For example, the way in which the rule of law works allows one to argue in favor of a new fundamental right, in addition to those mentioned by the Constitution. This argument rests on a two-fold claim: on the one hand, the American fundamental rights are not limited to the ones mentioned by the Constitution, and, on the other hand, all rights that qualify as inherent rights, for example, may become fundamental. The individual decision becomes thus justified, as the American Ronald Dworkin noted,[72] by its coherence within the "existing" law.[73] From your perspective, such decisional flexibility points out the commonality between the American legal system and the civil law system. The latter one thrives on this type of argument.

The ideals of morality and justice have also placed constraints on legal systems, and the American rule of law uses them as similar constraints too. For example, not all legitimate rules, which come through the proper channels, are or ought to be obeyed as law.

In fact, the rules that do not answer the ever-changing social circumstances are often not obeyed. In those situations, order and predictability depends on that society's ability to formulate new rules that are more apt to reflect those changes. In other words, another reason for updating your research is the changes in the

---

[72] R. DWORKIN, TAKING RIGHTS SERIOUSLY (1978).

[73] JURGEN HABERMAS, BETWEEN FACTS AND NORMS. CONTRIBUTIONS TO A DISCOURSE THEORY OF LAW AND DEMOCRACY 210 et seq. (discussing Dworkin's theory of law) (1996).

majoritiarian definition of justice or morality that might have caused new statutes to be enacted or different decisions to be issued.

From our first democratic beginnings, Americans believed that the people had a right to change the law when it seemed to them unjust. Legal theoreticians use that belief, for example, to explain the Americans' constitutional right to the judiciary (access to courts and to a jury of one's own peers).[74]

The rule of law inspires respect in our laws because it promotes more than social stability. It promotes justice, often regarded as "a matter of public interest."[75] However, often justice has been viewed as a procedural value, by contrast with arbitrary exercise of power. For example, the right to jury trials in criminal matters has been viewed as "a fundamental right, essential for preventing miscarriages of justice and for assuring that fair trials are provided for all defendants."[76]

It is interesting to note that while justice is easily accepted as a universal concept that transcends cultures, the rule of law has often been defined as local, because enforcing entities have traditionally been local. A cross-cultural definition of justice with which you may already be familiar resides with the Greek philosopher, Aristotle, in his *Nicomachean Ethics*.[77] Aristotle first spoke about distributive justice, which covers the way in which a society is organized, corrective justice, which helps understand the ways in which undesired changes to the social organization are corrected, retributive justice, which addresses the types of retribution a society favors, and commutative justice.[78]

---

[74] MORRIS R. COHEN, AMERICAN THOUGHT. A CRITICAL SKETCH 143 (1954).

[75] 7 TIMOTHY O. LENZ, CHANGING IMAGES OF LAW IN FILM AND TELEVISION CRIME STORIES 8 (2003).

[76] Duncan v. Louisiana, 391 U.S. 145, 158–59 (1968).

[77] ARISTOTLE, NICOMACHEAN ETHICS (D. Ross trans., 1925).

[78] *Id.* at 1129–34.

Talking about commutative justice, it should be said that the American views of what that is change dramatically in time. For example, property rules ensure that individuals (persons or corporations) can own property. While "highly deserving security,"[79] the revolutionary American politicians, like Wilson, also underlined that property should be a democratic end not a means in itself.[80]

Property rules change from one epoch to another, according to the majority's political views about what can be held as property. As detailed above, when Amendment 13 abolished slavery, the body of the American property rules changed dramatically. However, the individual nature of property rules did not change: private property remained the core of our property rules. Only the object of that ownership changed in order to adjust to the majority's views of what was moral to be held in property. Similarly, when the majority regards as immoral holding Mickey Mouse in quasi-perpetual copyright ownership, Congress will act accordingly, and adjust the copyright law to that view, and stop extending the copyright protection for Disney's monopoly over Mickey, Minnie, and Goofy.

This chapter briefly explained how law exists because humans need structured societies. Social order is achieved though concrete temporary rules that conform to each society's values. Each society develops its own constraints over legal norms. Those constraints mold legal norms so that they become an effective legal system that corresponds to the society's governing needs. When those needs change or disappear then the rules change or disappear, too. All legal norms have a clear role. They promote legitimate order. Legislative and administrative norms, as well as decisional law, govern our future and make sense of our conflict for today and tomorrow.

Of course, law depends on other enduring ideals as well. Prime among them are legality of rules and justice. However, while law aspires to be perceived as atemporal, you should avoid falling prey to such an assumption. Ultimately law is a social tool that has a

---

79 1 THE WORKS OF JAMES WILSON 30 (1804).

80 *Id.*

concrete role and a concrete lifespan, and, when it needs to be changed, it should be changed to avoid letting it become a social oppressor. Perhaps the Civil War could have been avoided if slavery rules had been abandoned and deemed illegal at an earlier phase in American history. For a researcher, the temptation to believe that law is atemporal may cause deficient studies. For a practitioner, such a belief produces incomplete results, and incomplete results are tantamount to professional malpractice.

American law is an abstract human construct to the extent that all law is an abstract human construct. However, its ideal of legitimate order rests on concrete legal norms that mirror specific societal needs. When they do not satisfy those needs anymore, and thus are unable to promote legitimate order, they are amended or replaced. The American legal system is thus dynamic, and understanding its dynamism helps you both strategize your studies and your legal research.

The next chapter will go a step further in explaining how the concrete, definite rules of law are created by legislation, judiciary, and administrative bodies. Thus, you will be able to identify the sources of American law, locate their repositories, find the specific legal norms you may want to research, and then update them.

Chapter 2
THE U.S. LEGAL SYSTEM AND ITS LAWMAKING INSTITUTIONS

A. THE U.S. LEGAL SYSTEM—A COMMON LAW SYSTEM

When we talked about American law as having an abstract and a concrete facet, we did it because clarifying its dual nature simplifies both the process of understanding how the U.S. legal system functions and how you are supposed to study and research it. For example, you come in touch with the abstract facet of American law when you study law as the code that steers political power into administrative power.[1] Furthermore, you come in contact with both the concrete and the abstract facet of the law when you study individual rights.

From a conceptual standpoint, individual rights can be viewed as powers of law conferred on the individual by the legal order through concrete legal norms, such as statutes or court decisions.[2] Those rights and the norms that confer them will inherently mirror the fundamental values of each society. Some of them are common to all societies (and legal systems) that have a similar cultural tradition, such as private property rights, while others will be specific to each society (and legal system) according to its contemporary needs and interests, such as welfare rights.[3]

---

1 For a discussion, *see* JURGEN HABERMAS, BETWEEN FACTS AND NORMS. CONTRIBUTIONS TO A DISCOURSE THEORY OF LAW AND DEMOCRACY (1996).

2 *Id.* at 85 et seq.

3 For a discussion about welfare entitlements in the American legal system, *see, e.g.*, Lucy Williams, *Welfare and Legal Entitlements: The Social Roots of Poverty*, *in* THE POLITICS OF LAW. A PROGRESSIVE CRITIQUE 569 et seq. (D. Kairys ed., 3d ed. 1982).

From a pragmatical point of view, individual rights go beyond their power of symbolism of empowerment. Rights are what you can do with them. For a member of the upper class, property rights surely have the making of a fundamental right. For a member of the underclass, expectedly so, things are totally different; such rights will have lesser value.

The U.S. legal system belongs to the common law tradition and it shares its principles and the core of its legal norms with the other common law systems. It is a development of the old English common law, which was aptly described as "the cumulative rules about law as expressed and altered from case to case, from precedent to precedent."[4] This official use of cases from precedent to precedent distinguishes it from the other legal systems, such as those that belong to the civil law tradition. Those officially deny any precendential value to court cases and theoretically rely only on parliamentary laws, usually collected in codes. Moreover, our sole reliance on laws whose majority come from different governmental lawmaking institutions, distinguishes our common law tradition—as well as the civil law one—from the various Islamic legal systems whose principal source of law is the Koran, or "the word of God as given to the Prophet."[5]

As you know, there are major differences among the legal systems that belong to the different traditions mentioned above. Moreover, differences can also be found between the American and the English system, despite their common law roots. For example, England has no written Constitution and, after the Glorious Revolution of 1688, the English Parliament became and has remained the supreme lawmaking institution in England, and it has been its duty to respect the inalienable rights of the individual. The United States has a written Constitution, which arguably divided the lawmaking duties among the three branches of the government, but it is through sheer common law precedent that we have established the Supreme Court as the supreme lawmaking

---

4 Beryl Harold Levy, Anglo-American Philosophy of Law. An Introduction to Its Development and Outcome 12 (1991).

5 Steven Vago, Law and Society 15 (5th ed. 1997).

institution in the United States. In the 19th century, in the famous case of *Marbury v. Madison*,[6] Chief Justice Marshall established the Court's prerogative—with regard to both statutes and case law—of declaring what constitutes binding law in the United States.

The American legal system is composed of many types of laws. Some are called substantive because they are perceived as substantially governing our behavior. Substantive laws are supposed to tell us what our rights and duties are, and we are expected to act accordingly. However, procedural rules do the same thing, with the only difference being that they regulate our behavior *vis-à-vis* the court system, where we go to protect our rights or clarify our duties. Another distinction has been between laws that govern our behavior *vis-à-vis* the state (public laws such as constitutional law) and laws that govern our behavior *vis-à-vis* each other and non-governmental entities (private corporations).

The distinction this book follows is that determined by the source of the legal norm: the lawmaking body that issues it. Statutory law, also known as legislation or "enacted law," is law made by legislatures. Case law, also known as decisional law or "judge-made" law, is law enacted by judges. Case law usually designates the decisions from intermediate (appellate) courts and courts of last resort. Finally, administrative law covers both rules issued by administrative bodies and decisions reached by them.

The next section may seem exceedingly simplistic by comparison to the previous one. It will cover the American lawmaking bodies both at the federal and state level. While the information covered there is already known to an American college student, it may be surprisingly new to you. It will provide you with the fundamental terminology you need to start your legal studies of American law. For the rest of this book we will focus on the concrete facet of American law. We will talk about the specific types of legal norms, about how they are created, how you can locate them, and, of course, how you can be sure that what you have located is still binding (good) law.

---

6 5 U.S. 137 (1863).

B. THE LAWMAKING BRANCHES OF THE GOVERNMENT

American law is a system of concrete rules that come from a variety of private and public sources. This chapter will focus on the public lawmaking institutions—the legislative, executive, and judicial branch. Those lawmaking institutions function both at the federal and state level.

This chapter will briefly describe how the legislative branch passes statutes, the judiciary branch adjudicates cases and controversies, and how the executive branch and administrative agencies issue rules and adjudicate disputes. If you understand how public law is created and where it is recorded, you will be able to effectively study and research the law of your interest. You will be able to identify the appropriate repositories of law and find what you need. Then you will be able to strategize the most effective way of comprehensively updating your research.

You know already that the U.S. government is a federation composed of 50 states. You may also know that the U.S. government is one of separated powers. The voice of the "pure, original fountain of all legitimate authority"[7] behind this government is the American people. However this fountain has an inherently ambiguous source, as it can be state legislations, federal legislation or the mob—the people itself. Eventually, this ambiguity became clarified: the sovereign people delegated the necessary power to govern to both the state and the federal government. If the people represent the source of legitimacy of public law, both at the federal and state level, nevertheless, the powers of the federal and the state government do not interfere. One of the Founding Fathers stated that "[t]he federal and State governments are in fact but different agents and trustees of the people, constituted with different powers, and designed for different purposes."[8]

---

7 A. Hamilton, *The Same Subject Continued (Other Defects of the Present Confederation)*, THE FEDERALIST No. 22, at 184 (L. Kramnick ed., 1987).

8 J. Madison, *The Influence of the State and Federal Governments Compared*, THE FEDERALIST No. 46, at 297.

Although separate, the governmental powers exercised through federal and state institutional structures are practically identical. Furthermore, they are open to identical congressional and judicial scrutiny. First, due to its internal—bicameral—organization, legislative bodies successfully make the tyranny of the majority impossible, and make the passage of unconstitutional statutes quasi-impossible. Then, as further detailed below, the judiciary exercises its control over both state and federal legislation every time an aggrieved party brings a lawsuit.[9]

1. Federal and State Legislatures

With one notable exception, Nebraska,[10] both the federal and the state legislative bodies are bi-cameral. For example, the New York legislative body is composed of the State Senate and Assembly.[11]

At the federal level, the two congressional chambers are called the Senate and the House of Representatives. Originally, the two chambers had different constituencies and bi-cameralism was supposed to diffuse the eventual tyranny of the majority (mob) and prevent it from legislating against the minority interests.[12] The majority was supposed to speak through representatives, and the minority through senators. Unless the two chambers agree on its content, as shown below, no statute can be enacted. Today, there are no institutional concerns regarding the original role of bi-cameralism—that of removing the legislative power from the mob.

---

9 For an in-depth treatment of federalism, *see* Akhil Reed Amar, *Of Sovereignty and Federalism*, 96 YALE L.J. 1425 (1986–1987).

10 *The Nation's Only Unicameral*, *at* http://www.unicam.state.ne.us/institute/citizen/main.htm. For a general view of the history of unicameralism in the United States, *see* JOHN MANNING, UNICAMERAL LEGISLATION IN THE STATES. (1938).

11 ELLEN GIBSON, NEW YORK LEGAL RESEARCH GUIDE I-28 (2d ed. 1998).

12 J. Madison, *The Alleged Tendency of the New Plan to Elevate the Few at the Expense of the Many Considered in Connection with Representation*, THE FEDERALIST NO. 57, at 343–47.

Procedurally, there are still differences between the two chambers. While the number of state representatives changes after each census, and states with growing populations gain representation, each state has only two senators to represent its interests in the Senate. Thus, unlike representatives who represent a specific part of the state's constituency, each Senator represents the whole state. Additionally, while all the representatives are elected at the same time, only one third of the senators are elected at any given time.

From a lawmaking point of view, there are few differences between the two chambers.[13] Members of each one can introduce a bill that they want to become a law. A committee of that chamber will study the bill and recommend passage with or without changes. If it reports back to its chamber with recommendations, further action is taken, and the bill goes to the floor for debate. If the bill passes the debate, it is sent to the other chamber where similar debates are expected. When there are proposed amendments, both chambers of Congress must agree on them. When the houses cannot agree on the content of a bill, the bill is referred to a special committee whose role is to resolve differences between the two legislative houses on the wording of a bill. Unless a bill passes both houses in the same form, it cannot be sent to the President for further legislative action.

The President has a few options. The President can sign the bill into law. The President can do nothing. Then, if Congress is in session, the bill becomes law automatically after ten days. If Congress is not in session when the ten-day period expires, the bill does not become law. The President can also veto the bill. Then, unless Congress overrides the veto by a two-thirds vote of both houses, the bill does not become law either. Once the bill is signed into law, it becomes binding federal statutory law.

At the state level, the process is almost identical. A legislator introduces a bill, and then the bill is referred to the appropriate standing committee of the house where it was introduced.[14] When

---

13 *See* http://uscis.gov/graphics/services/natz/usstruct.pdf.

14 ELLEN GIBSON, NEW YORK LEGAL RESEARCH GUIDE I-27 et seq. (2d ed. 1998).

the bill passes both houses, it is sent to the governor's office. Like the President, a governor can sign bills into law, veto them, or take no action on them. Once the bill is signed into law, it becomes binding state statutory law.

2. Federal and State Courts

The U.S. court system is divided into federal and state courts.[15] Both at the federal and state level, the court system is structured hierarchically. At a minimum, it comprises two types of courts: trial courts and courts of appeal. These are courts of general jurisdiction and can hear any type of case or dispute between two parties. Their responsibility is to explain and interpret the laws and thus solve the litigants' claims on the rights guaranteed to them in the Constitution and by law.

a. Federal Courts

The Supreme Court is the highest court within the federal judiciary. It is the only court that was established by the Constitution. Congress can only determine its composition and jurisdiction. The Court reviews federal appeals and state appeals that bear on a federal issue. (See Fig. 4.)

As shown in Appendix I, the Circuit Courts of Appeals are a step below, and their establishment is provided both by the Constitution and later congressional statutes. Theoretically, federal appellate decisions can be further appealed to the U.S. Supreme Court,[16] but due to the limited number of *certiorari* the Supreme Court grants every year, an appellate ruling represents the final decision in most cases.

There are 12 regional circuits. They are organized geographically so that each circuit court of appeals serves more than one

---

15 *See* Appendix 1.

16 *See* Appendix 1, *at* http://www.uscourts.gov/outreach/structure.jpg and Appendix 2, *at* http://www.courts.state.ny.us/courts/structure.shtml.

Fig. 4
Supreme Court Glossary

- All Supreme Court judges are called justices.
  - Since 1868, the Court has consisted of nine justices: one "Chief Justice of the United States," and eight associate justices.
  - The number of justices has varied: the Court had as few as five and as many as ten.
- The Supreme Court reviews cases as a matter of right and of discretion. However, in practice, the Supreme Court reviews cases as a matter of discretion, by granting a writ of *certiorari*. *Certiorari* means "bring up the record."[17]
  - In 2001 the U.S. Supreme Court reviewed 2,210 petitions for a writ of *certiorari* (requests for review) and granted 82, less than 4 percent.[18]

state.[19] Each circuit has a court of appeals. For example, the Court of Appeals for the Second Circuit serves three states: Connecticut, New York, and Vermont.[20] Thus, New York is covered by the second regional circuit, and its intermediary court is called the Court of Appeals for the Second Circuit.

In addition there are specialized courts that can hear only appeals in specialized cases. For example, the Federal Circuit Court handles appeals that involve patents as well as appeals from the Claims Court and the Court of International Trade.[21]

---

17 WILLIAM BURNHAM, INTRODUCTION TO THE LAW AND LEGAL SYSTEM OF THE UNITED STATES, at 176 (1996).

18 JANE GINSBURG, LEGAL METHODS at 16 (2d ed. 2004).

19 *See* Emory School of Law, Macmillan Law Library, *Federal Courts Finder*, *at* http://www.law.emory.edu/FEDCTS/.

20 *Id.*

21 U.S. Courts, *at* http://www.uscourts.gov/courtsofappeals.html.

A court of appeals hears appeals from both the district courts located within its circuit, and from decisions of federal administrative agencies.[22] For example, the appeals of the federal administrative agency called The National Labor Review Board (NLRB), will be heard either by the court of appeals of the place of the violation or that of the place of the NLRB's headquarters.

Each court of appeals covers one or more district courts.The district courts are the lowest level of federal courts. There are 94 federal judicial districts. Each state, including the District of Columbia and Puerto Rico, is covered by at least one federal district. Three territories of the United States—the Virgin Islands, Guam, and the Northern Mariana Islands—have district courts that hear federal cases as well.[23] There are four district courts that cover New York. The federal district court that covers Manhattan is called the U.S. District Court for the Southern District of New York.[24]

The district courts are courts of general jurisdiction that can hear all cases under the federal Constitution or a federal statute and controversies between citizens of different states. They are not restricted by law to hear only disputes limited to a specific subject matter.

District (trial) courts are the place where a lawsuit is brought and tried. Aggrieved individuals (persons or corporations) file their complaints there, explaining both the factual and legal issues that entitle them to relief from the courts. The party against the lawsuit, the defendant, attempts to contradict the plaintiff's narrative. The defendant joins the plaintiff in court and presents evidence to persuade the fact finder, either the jury or the judge, about the factual issues at hand in the lawsuit. Upon hearing the evidence and the arguments made by each party's lawyer, the jury finds in favor of one of the parties, according to the instructions about the applicable law given by the judge.

---

22 *Id.*

23 For more information, *see* U.S. Courts, *at* http://www.uscourts.gov/districtcourts.html.

24 *See* http://www.nysd.uscourts.gov/.

District court decisions are open to changes in appeal. The appeal stage may involve two levels of scrutiny: one from an intermediary court and another from the court of last resort. At the federal level, the court of last resort is the Supreme Court. However, unlike in civil law countries, the appeal in the American legal system involves only a review of the law and not of the facts. Thus, the district court has the last word in factual matters. Additionally, in light of the very small number of appellate courts, it is obvious that only a small percent of the district court decisions are appealed. Thus, the reality is that often district courts hold the last word in questions of law as well.

Courts make law through the decisions they issue as part of well-argued opinions. As you will see in Chapter 3, opinions have a rigorous structure and through exercise one can identify their ruling. Usually federal case law designates the decisions that benefit of precedential value and come from appellate courts and the court of last resort. However, although depleted of precedential value, district court decisions, when not appealed, constitute the final law in a case and thus are worth recording and researching.

According to the level of the court that issues them, decisions differ in their authority to dictate future courts to follow the same decision in similar factual contexts. Their authority—precedential value—varies according to the doctrine of *stare decisis*, which is further detailed in Chapter 4.

b. State Courts

Each of the 50 states of the United States has its own system of courts, whose structure mirrors the federal court system. While the court nomenclatures differ from state to state, they follow the same common law principle like the federal court system. State decisions from the "lower" (or trial) courts have to follow the precedent established by similar decisions from higher ranking courts (appellate courts and courts of last resort).

In New York, disputes that involve state law—either statutory or case law—will be tried in trial courts, which are known as "Supreme

Courts." Those decisions can be appealed to the Appellate Divisions of the Supreme Court. The court of last resort in New York, unlike in most other states, is the Court of Appeals.[25]

All court opinions are collected in court reporters: federal court opinions are collected in federal reporters and state court opinions are collected in state and regional reporters. These are accessible in print and on line.

3. The Executive Branch. Independent Administrative Agencies

The executive branch has a significant lawmaking component both at the federal and the state level. The federal executive branch is headed by the President of the Untied States, and it is composed of the Vice President, the Cabinet, and, the independent agencies. Each has special powers and functions, and each is authorized to issue binding rules.

a. The President

The President is elected every four years from a limited pool of presidential candidates who are chosen by their political parties in the months before the election. Usually the election is between a Republican and a Democratic candidate, because the Republican and Democratic parties are the largest political parties in the United States.

It is worth noting that people in each state vote *indirectly* for their choice for President. The people only vote for the electors who form the electoral college. Each state has a well-established number of electors, which is the same as the number of representatives plus the number of senators representing the state in Congress. The electors will meet after the November election, and vote for the President. Their choice will echo that of the largest number of people in their state.

---

[25] *See* Appendix 2, *at* http://www.courts.state.ny.us/courts/structure.shtml.

After F.D. Roosevelt's presidential tenure, the Federal Constitution was amended to impose presidential term limits.[26] Accordingly, since 1951, a President may serve only two terms of four years.[27]

The President exercises considerable lawmaking powers. The President can exercise them either directly, by signing federal bills into law or vetoing them, enforcing the treaties of the United States, or indirectly, by appointing the Cabinet members, the heads of independent agencies, as well as the Supreme Court justices and the federal courts judges.

For example, Presidents govern by issuing executive orders. Through executive orders Presidents may establish administrative agencies for the purpose of administering a specific piece of legislation, or a specific social and economic problem. According to the presidential prerogatives decreed by Congress in Chapter 9, title 5 of the United States Code, for instance, President Nixon established the Environmental Protection Agency (EPA) in 1970 through a reorganization plan that consolidated several existing agencies.[28]

b. *The Vice President*

The Vice President presides over the Senate and votes in case of a tie. The Vice President becomes President if the President is disabled or otherwise cannot serve.

c. *The Cabinet*

The Cabinet, "a creation of custom and tradition dating back to George Washington's administration, functions at the pleasure of the President."[29] It includes the Vice President and the heads of

---

26 Amendment XXII—Presidential Term Limits—was passed by Congress on March 21, 1947, and then ratified on February 27, 1951.

27 *Id.*

28 3 U.S.C.C.A.N., 91st Cong., 2d Sess. (1970).

29 OFFICE OF THE FEDERAL REGISTER. NATIONAL ARCHIVES AND RECORDS

the executive departments, which usually are called Secretaries. Those departments carry out government policies that ensure the functioning of our government.

During George Washington's Presidency, there were only four Cabinet members: Secretary of State, Secretary of Treasury, Secretary of War, and Attorney General; today, under George W. Bush's Presidency there are 15 such departments. (See Fig. 5.) Cabinet members are similar to European ministers who form any given government. Additionally, President George W. Bush has accorded Cabinet-level rank to other administrators. They are: the Administrator, Environmental Protection Agency; Director, Office of Management and Budget; the Director, National Drug Control Policy; and the U.S. Trade Representative.[30]

d. Independent Agencies

The independent (administrative) agencies differ from departments. First, their scope is more limited in substance. Second, at least theoretically, they are intended to be temporary.[31]

Administrative agencies are the result of an ever-expanding government that tries to represent as many interests as possible. Their role is to deal with a complex existing or rising social and economic problems. As a result, often, they both issue binding rules of general application and solve particular disputes within their jurisdiction.

For example, if big business necessitated the Securities and Exchange Commission (SEC), then "burgeoning labor and its troubles with business resulted in the National Labor Relations

---

ADMINISTRATION, THE UNITED STATES GOVERNMENT MANUAL, at 87 (2004/2005).

30 President Bush's Cabinet, *at* http://www.whitehouse.gov/government/cabinet.html.

31 For a list of current federal agencies, *see* Federal Agencies and Commissions, *at* http://www.whitehouse.gov/government/independent-agencies.html.

Fig. 5
The Cabinet

No.	Department	Functions (examples)
(1)	Department of State	Negotiates treaties and agreements with other countries
(2)	Department of the Treasury	Advises the President on financial matters
(3)	Department of Defense	Is responsible for national defense
(4)	Department of Justice	Represents the United States in all legal matters
(5)	Department of the Interior	*Inter alia*, identifies, protects, and restores endangered species of fish, wildlife, and plants
(6)	Department of Agriculture	Provides loans to help family-size and smaller farms
(7)	Department of Commerce	Is in charge of commercial issues, including patents
(8)	Department of Labor	Administers labor laws to ensure safe and healthful working conditions
(9)	Department of Health and Human Services	Administers assistance programs, such as Social Security
(10)	Department of Housing and Urban Development	Provides low-interest loans to promote home ownership and development of low-cost housing
(11)	Department of Transportation	Enforces safety transportation regulations
(12)	Department of Education	Administers educational programs
(13)	Department of Energy	Regulates energy rates and grants licenses
(14)	Department of Homeland Security	Is in charge of securing the homeland from terrorist attacks
(15)	Department of Veterans Affairs	Administers health care services, benefits programs, and national cemeteries for America's veterans and dependents

Board (NLRB)."[32] In light of their purpose, administrative agencies are authorized to implement their enabling statute or presidential order.

Accordingly, they issue rules and regulations, and sometimes even solve disputes that arise within their jurisdiction.

For example, the Environmental Protection Agency (EPA) acts under several enabling statutes.[33] Its lawmaking functions include both adopting rules and regulations, which further detail environmental statutes, and initiating litigation to promote the statutory standards established by those statutes, such as those provided by the Clean Air Act of 1955 and Safe Drinking Water Act of 1978. The creation of the Federal Trade Commission (FTC) was enabled by the Federal Trade Commission Act of September 1914. Its purpose is to promote fair competition in the economy, by instituting anti-trust cases and intervening in consumer and business affairs.[34] The NLRB was created by the National Labor Relations Act of 1935. It is among the most important administrative agencies "not only because of its widespread effect on administrative law, but also because of its major role in making and implementing national labor policy."[35] Finally, another major agency is the SEC, which was created by the Securities and Exchange Act of 1934, out of a national need to curb fraudulent stock and investment practices after the Great Crash of 1929.[36]

Similarly, at the state level, the executive branch is in charge of implementing state legislation. Furthermore, the governors, not unlike the President, function as "catalytic agents in the legislative process"[37] by structuring support through interest groups and

---

32 GOVERNMENT AGENCIES xxvi (Donald R. Whitnah ed., 1983).

33 *Id.* at 184 et seq.

34 *Id.* at 243 et seq.

35 *Id.* at 338 et seq.

36 *Id.* at 474 et seq.

37 STEVEN VAGO, LAW AND SOCIETY 125 (1997).

party leaders for different pieces of legislation within the legislative bodies. Additionally, it should be noted that at the local level too, the executive branch is complemented by state agencies in charge of dealing with existing or rising social and economic problems statewide.[38]

C. CONCLUSION

This chapter identified the lawmaking bodies of American public law. Later on you will learn how they work and where and how you can find the product of their rulemaking and decisionmaking authority.

By now you know that the U.S. legal system has the same social, economic, political, and moral constraints as any other legal system, and that the function of the American legal system is to promote legitimate order according to the core cultural values of individual liberalism. While the core cultural values remain the same, society and the way it understands them change. Thus, the American legal system is dynamic within well-established limits: those imposed by the rule of law. Understanding these idiosyncrasies will help you to adjust quicker to the American mode of studying and researching the law.

Next let's take a more in-depth look at each type of public norm—legislation, case law, and administrative law. You know that they are all open to judicial and congressional scrutiny. You also know that they survive it only if they are the result of legitimate exercise of public authority and their content does not violate the requirements imposed by the rule of law. Next, you will learn how they differ, and how that affects your studies and legal research. For example, you will see that judicial and congressional scrutiny happen differently for each type of norm, and that will affect the way in which you will strategize your studies and research.

---

38 For a list of all state agencies, *see* http://www.statelocalgov.net/.

APPENDIX 1
THE STRUCTURE OF THE FEDERAL JUDICIARY

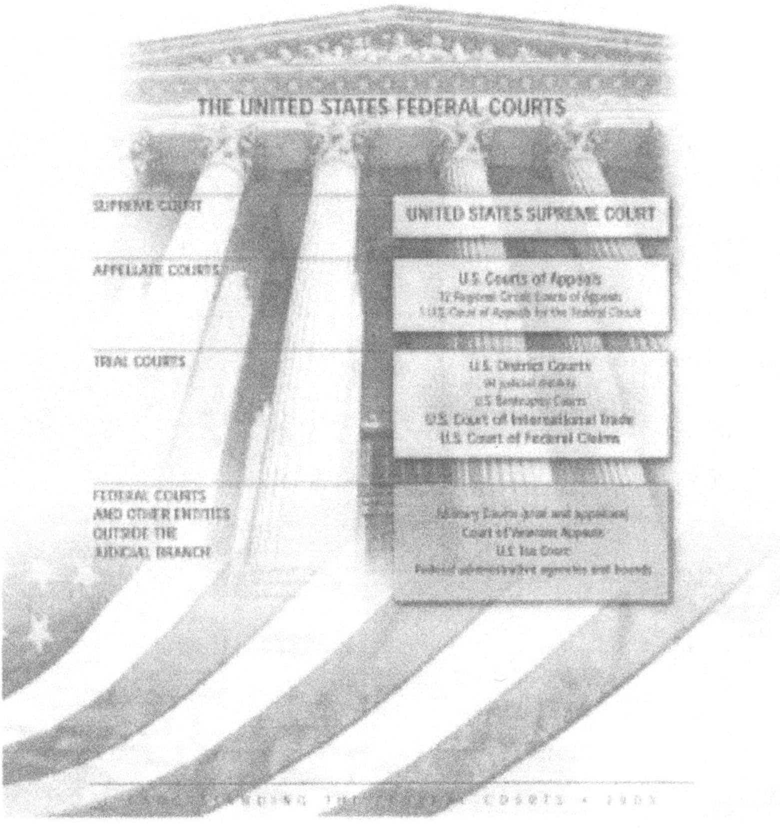

APPENDIX 2
THE STRUCTURE OF THE N.Y. STATE JUDICIARY

CIVIL COURT STRUCTURE

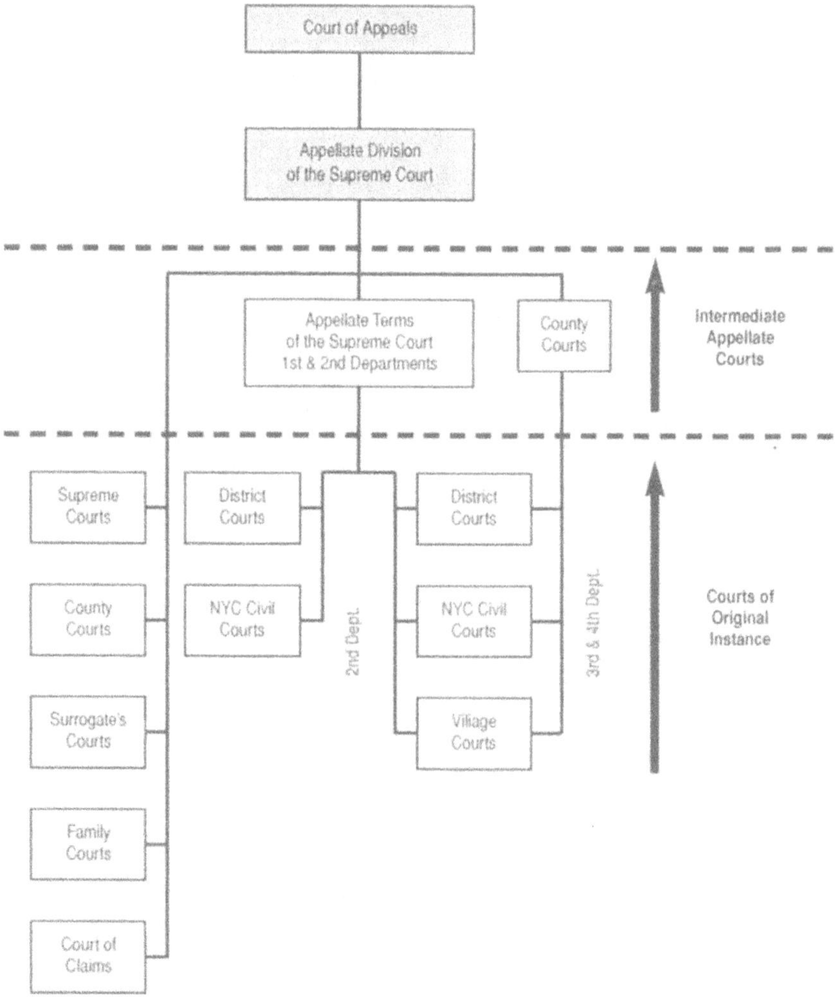

CRIMINAL COURT STRUCTURE

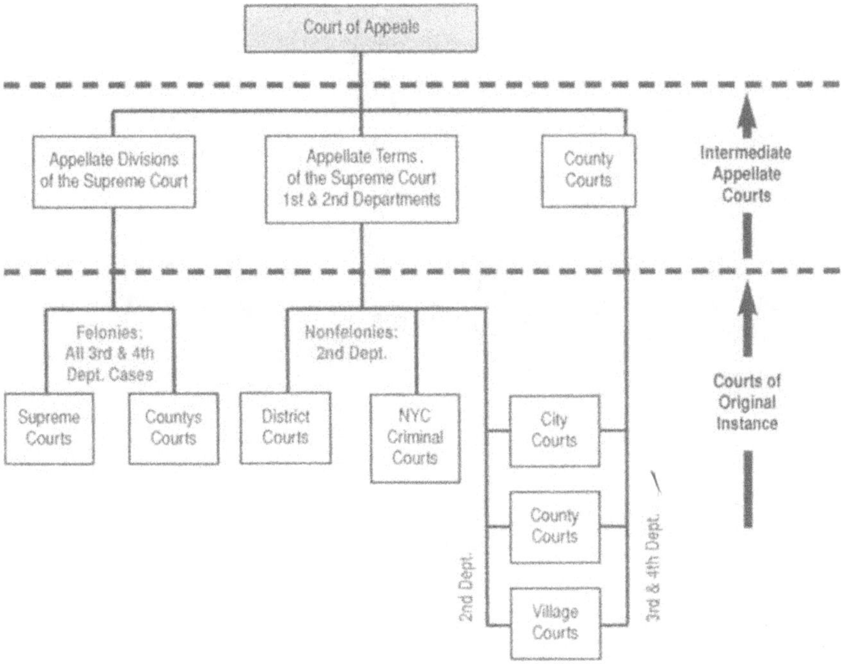

Chapter 3
Basic Principles of Legal Research

A. INTRODUCTION

Chapters 1 and 2 explained American law as a human construct, which aims to promote legitimate order through its myriad of concrete temporal norms. Those norms may be public or private. The public norms are: legislation, decisional, or administrative law. Chapters 1 and 2 also gave you a sense of how American law emerges and works.

They identified the institutions of pubic lawmaking. It became apparent that all three branches of the government make law both at the federal and at the state level, although lawmaking powers may not be expressly provided for in either the federal Constitution or its state counterparts.

The federal Constitution states that all legislative powers are vested in Congress (Article I, Section 1),[1] and that the judicial power vested in the Supreme Court covers cases and controversies (Article III, Section 2).[2] Indeed, legislatures, through elected representatives, whether in Congress, State Assemblies or City Councils, enact statutes.

The judicial branch—the federal and state court system—is responsible for solving specific disputes. However, in the process of applying the law and solving a dispute, courts make law. Each decision, through the doctrine of *stare decisis*, will further govern

1 *See* CONSTITUTION OF THE UNITED STATES AND THE DECLARATION OF INDEPENDENCE, POCKET EDITION. (21st ed. 2003) (H. Doc. 108-96), *available at* http://frwebgate.access.gpo.gov/cgi-bin/getdoc.cgi?dbname=108_cong_documents&docid=f:hd096.pdf.

2 *Id.*

similar cases in the lower courts within the same jurisdiction. Furthermore, the way in which a court applies a statute becomes the way we ask the next court to interpret and apply it. We can say that the meaning of a statute is given by a court.

The executive branch also makes law. While it is theoretically charged with enforcing the statutes, in doing so it issues its own legally binding rules. The President, like all state governors, issues executive orders. The federal and state agencies issue specific regulations that further detail the rules contained in their enabling statutes. Additionally, upon private complaints, agencies may conduct quasi-trials, which are called hearings, and issue decisions, which are similar to a court's decisions.

Learning about law is also learning to research its specific norms. You may have different interests that will prompt you toward learning about American law, but notwithstanding them, there are specific principles that apply to any legal studies and research endeavor. They will be further discussed here.

First, researching the U.S. legal system rarely is a simple task. You already know that law is often written in a jargon that is not user-friendly, and the most effective way to be sure that you found what you want is by identifying a "secondary source" or a commentary on that rule that will explain it to you. Before you start searching for a specific rule—a primary source—you should find a commentary about it.

When you next start your hunt for the primary source, do not forget that there are multiple repositories of primary sources that contain it. According to the information you have when you start your search, you will be better advised to use specific legal repositories. Additionally, depending on your resources and your specific needs, your choices may be limited, and especially from outside the United States, your search may be circumscribed to electronic databases.

The final step of any legal research is making sure that what you have finally found is still good law. For example, if you use the free electronic databases, such as the official, government-sponsored, databases, you should know that their coverage is limited. While they may have the most recent statutes, they may not have the one that answers your question. Additionally, they may not cover all court opinions that you would otherwise find by using the fee-based electronic databases Westlaw and Lexis, where the result often is only a click away.

B. DEFINING THE ROLE OF PRIMARY SOURCES

Primary sources—the legally binding rule or, as other authors have identified them, the official pronouncement of the governmental lawmakers[3]—represent the tangible aspect of American law, and the main object of your leal research. Statutes are the primary source of law that comes from the legislature—statutory law. Statutes are compiled in various statutory collections, which can be accessed in different ways, according to the information needed. Case law is the primary source of law that comes from courts—decisional law. Case law can be found in the compilations of court opinions. Administrative law is the primary source of law that comes from the executive branch and administrative agencies. Administrative law can be found in the compilations of presidential executive orders, those of administrative rules and regulations, and the compilations of administrative decisions.

All compilations of primary sources are publicly available whether in print or electronically within certain limits. Some are available for a fee while others are available free-of-charge. However, before you start choosing a specific repository, you are better off trying to identify a secondary source that will clarify that rule for you.

The next section will tell you about finding the appropriate clarifying secondary source. Furthermore, it will delineate the difference between the use of secondary sources by a legal practitioner and by someone who is not yet practicing law in the United States.

---

3 Morris L. Cohen & Kent C. Olsen, Legal Research in a Nutshell 7 (8th ed. 2003).

C. DEFINING THE ROLE OF SECONDARY SOURCES

Secondary sources are texts that explain the law. Secondary sources in American law do not share the unique pervasive role "la doctrine" or "la dottrina" has in both international law and in civil law systems. While doctrine, which should not be confused with either legislation or judicial decisions, by virtue of being the product of writings of professors and other scholars, nevertheless, strongly influences legislators and judges.

In American law, secondary sources have a lesser role, as they may persuade judges to accept a certain interpretation of a statute versus another one. Typically, their role is that of a tool used to identify the law as stated in its primary sources. For legal practitioners, secondary sources are useful because they are both a finding aid (similar to indexes) and a supplement to primary sources.

Legal practitioners look at a secondary source in a different way than a non-practitioner. Secondary sources help them start the legal research process, and may help them frame a legal argument when they present their client's case in front of a judge. When practitioners cannot find a binding primary source, then they look for sources of persuasive authority. Sources are only persuasive when they are not binding and cannot influence a court directly. They persuade the judge by their reasoning. Court opinions from other jurisdictions and secondary sources are also only persuasive.

For a legal practitioner, secondary sources will rarely represent the end of the legal research process. By their very essence, they are a commentary on specific legal rules, and not the law itself. Thus, a practitioner cannot simply rely on them giving a client legal advice. She runs the risk of becoming liable for malpractice for ignoring the most recent legal developments in that area. Depending on your own interests, you have to be aware of the timeliness flaw that secondary sources present by their very nature.

Secondary sources, which summarize, restate, review, analyze, and interpret the law, may often represent both the beginning and the end of your legal research process. For example, if you write

Fig. 6
Why You Should Start Your Legal Research with Secondary Sources

The right secondary source will answer all the following questions and many more.

- How do you know whether there is a statute that will be responsive to your question?
    - When does legislation have binding authority?
- How do you know whether the statute you had in mind has not been declared unconstitutional?
- How do you know the meaning of that statute?
- Can you ignore what a court had to say?
    - When would previous case decisions be binding upon a later one?
    - Remember the doctrine of *stare decisis.*
- Can you ignore what an administrative decision ruled?

a paper about the New York law regarding non-criminal "unconscious aiding and abetting," then reading a law review article, often identified as 16 TOURO L. REV. 25 (1999), could offer you the information you need.[4]

1. Before You Research, Make Sure that You Understand the Terminology: Legal Dictionaries

Depending on how versed you are in American law, a legal dictionary may be the first secondary source you need before tackling your legal query. Aside from English legal jargon, American law still contains Latin phrases, which need specific translations. For example, our writ of *certiorari*—through which the Supreme Court decides to review lower courts' decisions—comes from the Latin *certiorari* which means, according to *Black's Law Dictionary*, "to be more fully informed."[5] Whether knowing its Latin meaning

---

4 Dana Neacşu, *Concert of action by substantial assistance: what ever happened to unconscious aiding and abetting?*, 16 TOURO L. REV. 25 (1999).

5 BLACK'S LAW DICTIONARY 242 (8th ed. 2004).

helps you understand how the institution functions may be arguable. Nevertheless, using a dictionary the majority of the American lawyers use gives you confidence that you use American legal terminology correctly, too.

Aside from *Black's Law Dictionary*, which remains the most reputable source of legal definitions, there are other legal language reference works. Some of them are more modest in content. They are focused on a specific legal area, such as Lee's *Dictionary of Environmental Legal Terms*, which defines the terms according to the specific environmental legal rule that contains them. For example, "acid rain program" is defined according to the administrative regulation that established it, 40 C.F.R. Section 72.2 (2002), as "the national sulfur dioxide and nitrogen oxides air pollution control and emissions reduction program."[6]

2. Before You Research, Make Sure that You Understand the Citation: Citations Guides

Often the identifier for both a secondary or primary source is a condensed citation, such as the ones mentioned above: 16 TOURO L. REV. 25 or 40 C.F.R. Section 72.2 (2002). Like all legal citations, these also succeed in identifying both the type of document, the collection where it is located, and the specific document itself within the collection.

The 16 TOURO L. REV. 25 refers to a secondary source. More precisely it identifies an article that was published in the 16th volume of the *Touro Law Review* at page 25.

The *Code of Federal Regulations* (C.F.R.) part of the second citation identifies both the type of document and the collection where it is located. It tells you that the document in question is a primary source. It is an administrative regulation, which is contained in the C.F.R.

By identifying the type of document, the citation tells the reader how much weight the document carries: as a secondary source, it

6 C.C. LEE, DICTIONARY OF ENVIRONMENTAL LEGAL TERMS 5 (1997).

will always be only persuasive, and, as a primary source, it requires further investigation. For example, the document in our example is an administrative regulation. You know exactly how important such a source is in your research. As in your own legal system, administrative documents carry less authority than statutory and decisional law in American law as well.

Furthermore, the C.F.R. citation identifies more than the type of source: administrative regulation. It identifies the very administrative rule contained in that document itself. The number that precedes the abbreviation, "40" indicates the title of the U.S. Code (a codification of all U.S. laws broken down by subject matter) to which the administrative regulation relates (*e.g.*, title 40 concerns environmental protection), while the number that follows the abbreviation, "72.2," indicates the section number of the regulation. The year, "2002," is the last time that regulation was updated. Thus, although you may not know its name, you know its address, so it will be easy to locate once you choose the repository of administrative regulations you want to use: in print or online.

There are a few sources that would help you make sense of any legal citation. Peter Martin's *Introduction to Basic Legal Citation*[7] is easily accessible online. However it is not meant to be comprehensive. It does not cover the meaning of every single abbreviation of American law sources: either primary or secondary. Edited by Mary M. Price, assistant director of the Law Library at Vanderbilt Law School, *Bieber's Dictionary of Legal Abbreviations,* however, provides extensive coverage of all legal abbreviations within the U.S. legal system. It thus helps you understand the abbreviations for titles, terms, and names used in American legal literature.

It is worth noting that legal professionals often use the *Bluebook: A Uniform System of Citation.* The need for the *Bluebook* is dictated by the need to be uniform when citing legal sources that support arguments used in court papers, such as legal memoranda, etc. In addition to citation rules, the *Bluebook* is also useful because it lists

---

7 *See* http://www.law.cornell.edu/citation/.

all federal and state primary sources, and identifies them both by their full title and their legal abbreviations. For example, if you are interested in learning the name of the repositories that cover the Supreme Court decisions, all you need to do is go to the section of the *Bluebook* called the "Table on United States Jurisdiction" (T.1) and search for the names of the Supreme Court reporters. In addition to their names, you will also learn the time frame covered. For example, just by using the *Bluebook*, you find out that the name of one of the reporters is the *United States Reports*, that it covers all opinions starting with those decided in 1790, and that its abbreviation is "U.S."

D. IDENTIFYING SECONDARY SOURCES

If you know that you have a good grasp of the issues in question, and that you understand them sufficiently that searching for secondary sources will be meaningful and bring you a responsive source that covers your topic, then the next step is to learn how you can locate those commentaries about the law. We will start with treatises and then move on to articles, whether or not they are published in law reviews and journals.

1. Treatises and Other Legal Monographs

Legal practitioners will use a treatise when the research fits within a traditional area of legal doctrine. Aside from its practicality, the mere reference to a well-known treatise will lend professional prestige to their papers. Treatises are books written by well-established members of the legal academe. For example, mentioning *Nimmer on Copyright* signals to the judge that the attorney who authored that brief is more knowledgeable and sophisticated in copyright issues than the one who omitted that specific reference.

Anybody who is not comfortable with a specific legal area should first try to see whether their area of interest is covered by a treatise, because treatises have the advantage of explaining issues in a larger context. For example, those of you interested in public nuisance will be in a better position starting with a treatise on torts, such as *Prosser and Keeton on the Law of Torts,* which will explain the different types of nuisance by emphasizing their differences. Next, those of you interested in environmental law will find it easier when you move to a more specialized environmental treatise, such as Grad's *Treatise on Environmental Law,* to understand why public nuisance has become an environmental tort as well.

Treatises are extremely useful in our legal system because they summarize court decisions, and give you an insightful view of the development of our common law system based on a complex interplay of court decisions, statutes, and administrative regulations. While all treatises are useful, those usually identified as "hornbooks" are of special value because they are written for students, albeit law students, and not legal practitioners. Like Prosser's *Law of Torts,* they are more likely to give an overview of the area in a more comprehensive way. Similarly useful, for those who need to learn fast about a legal subject, are those treatises published by West in its *nutshell series.* For example, if you are interested in a quick and reliable overview of the U.S. patent system, Miller and Davis's *Intellectual Property: Patents, Trademarks, and Copyright in a Nutshell* will be the right place to start your search.

As the trend towards digitization continues, more and more secondary sources are available through Lexis and Westlaw. For example, if *Nimmer on Copyright* is available from Lexis, other copyright secondary sources are available from Westlaw. Both Lexis and Westlaw have searching features similar to the field search offered by any library catalog. For example, if you know the title of the treatise you want to locate you may do so through "Find a Source" on Lexis, or "Find a Database Wizard" on Westlaw.

Although not treatises, legal monographs, which talk about important doctrinal aspects, are also useful in deciphering a specific area of law. For example, George Fletcher's *Basic Concepts of Legal thought,* is an excellent introductory tool to understanding how American jurists perceive legal thinking.

2. Law Review Articles

If your efforts in identifying a specific treatise fail, the next step should be finding a law review article that expounds on the primary source of your interest. Those articles are authored by members of the academe, practitioners, and law students. They follow a well-established practice of analyzing and discussing the chosen topic so that the reader can get an accurate view of what the law is in the very specific and often quite narrow area that constitutes the topic of that article.

Law review articles, or law journal articles, have the advantage of covering obscure areas in more detail than a treatise. For example, if Prosser's *Law of Torts* explains the different standards for concert of action by substantial assistance, it does not explain state law subtleties. To the contrary, a law review article, such as Neacşu's *Concert of Action by Substantial Assistance: What Ever Happened to Unconscious Aiding and Abetting?* will devote its entire content to explaining that issue according to a specific state law, New York law.

If treatises have the advantage of explaining the law that covers a larger body of legal norms—torts, environmental law, criminal procedure, etc.—then law review articles, have the advantage of advocating a point of view that may be similar to that of the reader, and thus offer ready-made support for an argument. Treatises mostly refrain from challenging any given *status quo*.

E. FINDING SPECIFIC SECONDARY SOURCES

Secondary sources may be located using electronically available tools. Treatises may be located through online library catalogs. Law review articles may equally be located using a variety of cataloging tools: legal indexes. Because the strategy used for each type of secondary source is different, they will briefly be explained below.

1. Treatises

The strategy for finding a treatise is different than the one for finding a responsive law review article. You can find treatises by using a library catalog or even Google Scholar. (See Fig. 7.) All major library catalogs are available online. The first step is to locate a library, and then its online catalog. Then, you will have to use your basic research skills in finding any books in any online catalog. You limit your search in the "Title" field when you are sure of your title. If you know only the subject matter, then do your search in the "keyword" or "word" field. Avoid the search option in the "Subject" field, because the choices within that field are restricted to a controlled vocabulary according to the subject headings designated by the Library of Congress.

Once you find a list of sources, it is not very complicated to discern which one you would like to consult first. As mentioned before, only well-established members of the academe publish treatises, including the West series called "nutshells," and even fewer publish hornbooks.

Unless you are interested in the historical treatment of a legal area, you should always start your search with the most recent edition of a treatise. The most recent edition of a treatise offers a much needed survey of the law that will bring your search up-to-date. Thus, the date of publication should be a search strategy that you may want to use to limit your results.

2. Law Review Articles

There are thousands of law review articles published yearly. Unlike authors of treatises who are limited by their small profession, the academe, there is no such limit when it comes to authors of law review articles. They can be members of the academe, practitioners, or even students.

Because of their gigantic number, law review articles cannot and are not cataloged in any library catalog. There are fee-based electronic databases that either index or contain the full text of recent law review articles.

The best approach to a manageable and reliable search of law review articles is by using a legal index. The *Index to Legal Periodicals*

Fig. 7
Finding a Treatise

1. Go to Google:
   - http://www.google.com/
- Find a local law school library:
   - http://www.law.columbia.edu/home
- Go to their online catalog:
   - http://pegasus.law.columbia.edu/
- Find if they have a treatise on torts
   - Choose the search option "WORDS in Corporate Author, Title, or Subject"
   - Then Type "torts" and "treatise" as a search word
   - Limit your search by additional fields
     e.g., the date of publishing
     Dobbs's *The Law of Torts*.

Or

2. Go to "Google Scholar"
   - http://scholar.google.com
   - Search for scholarly literature on torts.

and Books, which is part of a database known as Wilson's Web, is the most commonly used legal index. It is usually available from many universities' database Web sites, as well as from the prestigious fee-based electronic databases Westlaw and Lexis.

The advantage of using an index is that you only obtain results that discuss your issue in depth, as opposed to the results you obtain from a full-text database, which may only mention your research terms in passing in a footnote. For example, if you search for articles on the "tragedy of commons," you will obtain 19 results that have the advantage of going back in time for almost two decades and cover in-depth treatment of your issue in varied areas: from environmental law to international law and intellectual property.

Once you identify the articles through the index, you have a choice for your next step. You may retrieve those documents either from the in-print version of the law reviews, or from their electronic version, through Westlaw, Lexis, or its more limited version, LexisNexis Academic Universe. Westlaw also has a similar, more limited, product.

While many of you have already heard of Westlaw and Lexis, few know about LexisNexis Academic Universe. This database is usually offered through any university's database system. It gives you the option of finding an article by searching in the following fields: "full-text." "author," "citation," and "title." Additionally, you may be able to limit your search by the date of its publication, such as the "previous six months," etc. Westlaw's similar product, which is offered from many universities' databases, can be used in a similarly intuitive manner.

However, a full-text database is not the best first step when you do not know too much about the topic, or when the topic is either fashionable or of popular interest. Then you will obtain too many results and it is hard to handle the hits in a meaningful way. If you try to limit it by the date of the publication you may eliminate your seminal results without even knowing it.

Returning to the previous example about the "tragedy of commons," using a full-text electronic database as your first step in locating law review articles will be unfortunate. You obtain too many hits, although the law review articles database goes back only to the 1980s. For example, a search within the entire LexisNexis Academic Universe library of law review articles could not be performed because it brought up over 1,000 documents.

The "tragedy of the commons" was coined in the 1960s, so if you were to limit your search to articles published within the previous six months, such an arbitrary limit is unreliable. Thus, the 55 hits a search performed on November 16, 2004, brought up are highly questionable. Then, how do you know how to manage your search in a meaningful way?

One way will be to go back to a library catalog and see if you can find a monograph about the tragedy of commons, which will inform you about what is considered to be seminal literature in this area or who is considered to be the specialist in this area. You can perform this search in public library catalogs as well as in general studies and law library catalogs. They will all provide reliable sources that contain historic information.

Then, you may want to go back to the full text database offered by either electronic service that was mentioned above, and use it only for the most recent articles. Another way of managing the results from a full-text database is learning about the different authors' credentials. A quick Google search will provide you with sufficient information.

If full-text databases may not be the best first step in your search for law review articles, nevertheless they may be excellent retrieving sites, when you have all the information you need to locate an article. For example, if you look for Eben Moglen's *Considering Zenger: Partisan Politics and the Legal Profession in Colonial New York*, and you know either its title or its citation—94 COLUM. L. REV. 1495 (1994)—going to Lexis, Westlaw, or even to their more limited versions, such as LexisNexis Academic, is the most efficient way of locating it. However, if you are interested in the article on concert of action, knowing its citation—16 TOURO L. REV. 25 (1999)—you may not find it by simply going to any of these databases.

While Lexis and Westlaw have more complete coverage than LexisNexis Academic, neither is totally comprehensive. Even when they cover a title, they may not cover all the issues published by that law review, but only the most recent ones. Indeed, Lexis contains only the most recent volumes of the *Touro Law Review*, while Westlaw happens to contain all of them.

Thus, when you know the author or the title of a not-so-recent article, another fee-based electronic database, HeinOnLine, usually offered through law school libraries' databases, may be a better source than either Lexis or Westlaw. However, you should be aware of its own coverage limits. HeinOnLine's licensing agreements involve a "moving wall," which makes available only law review articles from the first issue prior to a set number of years before the present date. Thus, only through complementary use of either Westlaw or Lexis and HeinOnLine should offer comprehensive access to all American law review articles.

Finally, on occasion, you may be able to locate articles that have been published in law reviews through the World Wide Web as well. One such example is Moglen's article, *Considering Zenger*, which is freely available on the Internet,[8] and which you can obtain by doing a basic Google search.

3. Articles on Legal Topics on the World Wide Web

Using Google, you may locate useful contextual information about a primary source. The major problem remains reliability. How reliable are the sources you can locate through Google?

It all depends on the means used to locate that information. There are specialized portals, such as FindLaw, or SSRN that may provide you access to legal information authored by legal practitioners, or even law professors. Some authors, such as Eben Moglen in the intellectual property field, have their own Web sites. From there you can link to their papers. Additionally, as mentioned before, Google Scholar[9] functions as a catalog of scholarly literature, which includes theses, articles, preprints, as well as abstracts and scholarly articles available across the Web.

a. FindLaw: FindLaw Professionals: Summaries of Law

FindLaw—available at http://www.findlaw.com—is an electronic service that offers access to commentaries about law authored by "FindLaw Professionals." "FindLaw Professionals" present themselves as a "group of well-respected authorities in their legal practice areas." Their legal summaries are advertised to help any "individual legal consumer" learn more about "the legal system

8 *See* http://emoglen.law.columbia.edu/publications/zenger.html.

9 *Available at* http://scholar.google.com.

and individual areas of the law." Indeed, if you take a look at the posted summary for copyright law, you see that the author is a law practitioner, Mark Radcliffe, partner in the law firm of Gray Cary Ware & Freidenrich LLP. The summary is not pretentious. It is easy to follow and it accurately covers the major issues regarding the U.S. copyright law.

b. *SSRN: A Recipient of Legal Secondary Sources*

The Social Science Research Network (SSRN—available at http://ssrn.com) is a good place to locate texts on current and obscure issues of law. SSRN is composed of a number of specialized research networks in social sciences, including law. The SSRN eLibrary consists of an Abstract Database—which houses abstracts on over 80,500 scholarly working papers and forthcoming papers—and which is available for free. The Electronic Paper Collection—which currently contains over 55,800 downloadable documents in pdf format—are often available for a fee.

Many of the works first made public through SSRN disappear when they are also published in a law review. However, even when the full text ceases to be available, the abstract of the paper and the citation of the published article remain available.

c. *Secondary Sources Accessible Through the Authors' Personal or Institutional Web Sites*

Once you have identified a useful secondary source, you may want to see whether that author wrote something else on the same issue. Depending on the type of source, treatise or law review article, you will use a different approach.

If it is a treatise, you revert to what we have said about searching a library catalog for a treatise. If it is an article, the best way to go about it is to use a specialized index and do an author and subject-matter search. If you do not have access to such an index, or to the fee-based databases mentioned above, the next best thing is to try to locate the author's personal or institutional Web site.

The ordinary search engine Google, available at http://google.com is the easiest way to locate such sites.

F. FINDING REPOSITORIES OF PRIMARY SOURCES: RESEARCH TECHNIQUES

Once you have accessed the contextual background information, you need to go a step forward and read the law itself: the statute, case law, or administrative rule or decision that governs your area of interest. The text of the law is often identified as the primary source.

In order to read the text of the law, you need to identify the collection that contains it and decide whether you want to see it in print or electronically. Sometimes that decision is driven by your financial resources.

Unlike other types of research, legal research is done in steps. The first step is identifying the type of legal norm you want to see: the Constitution, a federal or state statute, a federal or state court decision, or an administrative rule, regulation, or decision. The next step is identifying the collection, or the repository of primary sources, which contains such norms. Remember, that any given legal text, with very few exceptions, is found as part of a multitude of collections of similar legal documents. Furthermore, remember that all the sources identified here are also available either through Lexis or Westlaw.

Your research is not finished until you make sure that what you found is still the applicable law in that area. Remember that the role of the rule of law is to make sure that the U.S. legal system contains only norms that satisfy specific procedural and substantive requirements, such as legitimacy, and that the judicial branch is the means to ensure them. According to your financial resources, the updating step can be done in two ways. It can be done in a more tedious and not totally trustworthy way, which incorporates free-of-charge electronic sources, or in a more effective but fee-based way, which relies on either Lexis or Westlaw. If you end up practicing law in the United States, you will always want to use the fee-based databases.

1. Locating the Federal Constitution

The federal Constitution is our fundamental law. It is available by itself both in print as well as online.[10] It is available as part of the official federal statutory collections: the *United States Statutes at Large* commonly known as *Statutes at Large*,[11] and the *United States Code*. Using the specialized free-of-charge legal portal FindLaw, you can easily access the Constitution on line.[12] Of course, both Lexis and Westlaw contain the federal Constitution in their federal law library: *Federal Legal—U.S.* for Lexis and *U.S. Federal Materials* for Westlaw.

2. Locating Repositories of Federal Statutory Law

Federal statutes are available both in print and online. Because of their large number, statutes are officially collected chronologically, in the order they are passed by each Congress, and by subject matter, according to 50 subject matters identified numerically in 50 titles. The official chronological collection is called the *United States Statutes at Large* commonly known as *Statutes at Large*, and the official codified version, which contains federal statutes published by subject matter, is called the *United States Code*.

The *Statutes at Large* contains every law, public and private, enacted by Congress in order of the date of its passage from 1789. Each *Statutes at Large* volume is numbered sequentially. To access the entire collection of *Statutes at Large* you need to have access to both a library that carries the print collection, and to the Internet, in order to access the electronic collection. Please remember that *Statutes at Large* is not available in its entirety in a single format—either in print or electronically.

The print collection of the *Statutes at Large* does not contain the most recent statutes. The electronic version covers only the very

---

10 *See supra* note 2.

11 1 Stat. 10.

12 *See* http://www.findlaw.com/casecode/constitution/.

Fig. 8
Finding Primary Sources of Law: Research Steps

1. Using Secondary Sources, identify the type of document you want to see
   - the Constitution, or
   - a statute, or
   - a court decision, or
   - an administrative rule, regulation, or decision

2. Identify the appropriate repository of primary laws that contains that type of documents
   - Statutory compilations
   - Court reporters
   - Administrative compilations

3. Locate your document within the compilation
   - Use the citation you have
   - Use the collection's aiding tools (locators)

old and very recent statutes, including those that are not yet available in the print collection. The first 18 volumes of the *Statutes at Large*, which contain laws enacted from 1789 to 1875, are available from the Library of Congress's full-text electronic database.[13] Similarly, the volumes of the *Statutes at Large* collection which contain laws enacted after 1995, are available from GPO Access,[14] and the volumes that contain laws enacted after 1993 are available from the Library of Congress.[15]

Unlike the *Statutes at Large*, the *United States Code* contains the general and permanent laws of the United States organized by subject matter, according to 50 numbered titles. A title may be made up of a few volumes. For example, federal statutes on education are located in title 20 of the *United States Code*. Currently there are

---

13 *Available at* http://memory.loc.gov/ammem/amlaw/lwsllink.html.

14 *At* http://www.gpoaccess.gov/plaws/browse.html.

15 *At* http://thomas.loc.gov/.

six volumes of statutes that make up title 20. Moreover, unlike the *Statutes at Large*, the *United States Code's* function is more than recording federal statutes: it is to ensure easy access to the applicable law. Thus, it is periodically updated. Every six years there is a new edition of the Code. The 1994 and the 2000 editions are also available online from the full-text database offered by GPO Access, a service of the U.S. Government Printing Office.[16]

The *United States Code* is available electronically also from the Office of the Law Revision Counsel of the U.S. House of Representatives, which prepares and publishes the Code.[17] This database can be easily located with the help of a specialized portal, FindLaw, a free-of-charge service further described below.[18]

Of course, both Lexis and Westlaw contain federal statutes in their federal law library: *Federal Legal—U.S.* for Lexis and *U.S. Federal Materials* for Westlaw. Lexis covers statutes in their codified version, through the electronic format of its version of the United States Code, the *United States Code Service*, further detailed in Chapter 4. Westlaw covers statutes both in their sequential order and in their topical organization. Westlaw covers all public laws enacted by the U.S. Congress in three libraries. The older statutes, enacted from the first through the 92nd Congress are available in the *United States Statutes at Large 1789–1972*. Public Laws enacted during the first session of the 93rd Congress (1973) through the second regular session of the 107th Congress (2002), are available in the *United States Public Laws 1973–2002*. Finally, Public Laws passed during the current 108th Congress are available in the *United States Public Laws*. Additionally, Westlaw covers statutes in their codified version, through the electronic format of its version of the United States Code, the *United States Code Annotated*, further detailed in Chapter 4.

---

16 *At* http://www.gpoaccess.gov/uscode/index.html.

17 *See* http://uscode.house.gov/search/criteria.php.

18 *See* http://www.findlaw.com/casecode/uscodes/.

3. Locating Court Reporters: Repositories of Court Opinions

A court decision is usually included in the written opinion that marks the end of the legal dispute. Opinions have been collected in "court reporters" for hundred of years. Those reporters are available both in print—usually in a West publication—and electronically from Lexis and Westlaw.[19] In order to locate a specific reporter, first you need to know its name. The *Bluebook*—as mentioned before—is a useful tool in identifying the correct name of each reporter. Once you know its title, then you go to a library catalog and use it in the same way you use it to locate any other book.

Opinions are available electronically from different databases and through different portals. As shown below, LexisOne,[20] which is part of Lexis, offers access to all reported state and federal court opinions decided in the past five years, and to the Supreme Court cases from 1790 to present, free of charge.[21]

Recent opinions are available also from each court's Web site, and they can be accessed either by using a specialized portal, or by doing a Google search for the specific court. For example, FindLaw, which is part of Westlaw, is a portal that directs you to those Web sites. Additionally, as further detailed below, FindLaw also covers all the Supreme Court opinions from 1893 to present.[22]

A court's Web site is a very useful place to start locating opinions. For example, on the Supreme Court of the United States' site[23] you may find a list of electronic portals and databases that contain the Court's opinions,[24] the Court's recent opinions, as well

---

19 *See* https://web2.westlaw.com/.

20 *See* http://www.lexisone.com/.

21 *See* http://www.lexisone.com/lx1/caselaw/freecaselaw?action=FCLDisplayCaseSearchForm&l1loc=L1E.

22 *See* http://www.findlaw.com/casecode/supreme.html.

23 *See* http://www.supremecourtus.gov/.

24 *See* http://www.supremecourtus.gov/opinions/obtainopinions.pdf.

as mimeographed copies of 36 volumes of the official Supreme Court Reporter, the *United States Reports,* which cover opinions decided from 1991 to 2002.[25] Furthermore, the Court's site also contains a "Case Citation Finder," whose purpose is to help searchers obtain the proper citation of a Court's opinion, when they know the name of either party.[26] The role of a proper citation will be further detailed below.

Both Lexis and Westlaw contain federal case law in their federal law library: *Federal Legal—U.S.* for Lexis and *U.S. Federal Materials* for Westlaw. Lexis covers federal case law in the *Federal Court Cases—Combined* library. This library contains the U.S. Supreme Court cases from 1790 to present, the U.S. courts of appeal cases from 1789 to present and the U.S. district courts from 1789 to present. Similarly, Westlaw covers all federal court cases, in the *Cases & Judicial Materials* library.

4. Locating Repositories of Administrative Rules, Regulations, and Decisions

For more than half a century, federal administrative rules and regulations have been published in two official publications: The *Federal Register*, and the *Code of Federal Regulations.* Since 1936, the *Federal Register* has been the official daily publication of rules, proposed rules, and notices of federal agencies and organizations. Additionally it publishes executive orders and other presidential documents. Each year a new volume of the *Federal Register* is published. The current volume is 69. The last 11 volumes are available electronically from GPO Access,[27] and through FindLaw.[28]

It is worth noting that while the *Code of Federal Regulations* like the *United States Code* is divided into 50 topics; substantively, the

---

25 *See* http://www.supremecourtus.gov/opinions/boundvolumes.html.

26 *See* http://www.supremecourtus.gov/opinions/casefinder.html.

27 *See* http://www.gpoaccess.gov/fr/index.html.

28 *See* http://www.findlaw.com/casecode/fed_register.html and http://www.findlaw.com/casecode/cfr.html.

topics of the two codified compilations do not necessarily correspond. For example, the 17th topic in both compilations is called "title 17." However, in the *United States Code* title 17 covers statutes on copyrights, while in the *Code of Federal Regulations* title 17 covers rules and regulations on commodity and securities exchanges. Thus, if you are interested in learning how statutory provisions regarding copyright arbitration have been further detailed by administrative agencies, going to the C.F.R. volumes that cover title 17 would be a mistake. The rules and regulations regarding copyright arbitration are available in title 37 of the *Code of Federal Regulations,* which is entitled "Patents, Trademarks, and Copyrights."[29]

The *Code of Federal Regulations,* starting with some titles of the 1996 volume, is available electronically free of charge from GPO Access,[30] as well as through FindLaw.[31] Accordingly, you can view the topic each title covers since 1996 at GPO Access.[32]

Older administrative decisions of the federal government and federal agencies are available in print, while more recent ones are available electronically free-of-charge from their official Web site. For example, since 1942, the U.S. Department of Agriculture publishes the decisions issued by its administrative judges in *Agriculture Decisions.* Its post-2000 decisions are also available on its Web site.[33] However, the administrative decisions issued by both the Office of Hearings and Appeals of the Department of Education and the Secretary of Education are more difficult to find. Free-of-charge but limited access is available from the Department's official Web site.[34]

---

29 *Id.*

30 *See* http://www.gpoaccess.gov/cfr/index.html.

31 *See* http://www.findlaw.com/casecode/fed_register.html and http://www.findlaw.com/casecode/cfr.html.

32 *See* http://www.access.gpo.gov/nara/cfr/cfr-table-search.html#page1.

33 *See* http://www.usda.gov/da/oaljdecisions/.

34 *See* http://www.ed-oha.org/index.html.

To the extent federal agencies have the authority to solve disputes, their decisions are recorded also. The decisions issued by the U.S. Securities and Exchange Commission are available both in commercial as well as in official publications, in print—*Decisions and Report*—and electronically. For example, the Commission's Opinions and orders issued from 1996 onward are available electronically free-of-charge from its official Web site.[35]

Both Lexis and Westlaw contain both the *Code of Federal Regulations* and the *Federal Register* in their federal law library: *Federal Legal—U.S.* for Lexis and *U.S. Federal Materials* for Westlaw. Both Lexis's and Westlaw's coverage of the *Federal Register* starts with the *Federal Register* volume published in 1980. However, Westlaw contains historical volumes of the *Code of Federal Regulations* starting with the 1984 volume. Additionally, part of Lexis's main library—*Federal Legal—U.S.*—is the *Federal Agency Decisions, Combined.* It covers decision from all U.S. departments, as well as decisions from many federal agencies. Its time coverage varies. Moreover, both Lexis and Westlaw cover administrative decisions that are republished through various commercial publications published by either the Bureau of National Affairs (BNA) or Commerce Clearing House (CCH).

Federal administrative decisional law is also available through the official Web sites of each agency. However, their coverage is limited, as their electronic publication does not go back more than a few years.

G. IDENTIFYING SPECIFIC PRIMARY SOURCES WITHIN SPECIFIC LEGAL REPOSITORIES

Once you have identified the appropriate legal repository, you are closer to the end of your journey. The next step requires you to use correctly the information you had from the beginning and identify the very source that caused you this search. If you started with a citation, you need to translate it correctly. If you know the

---

35 *See* http://www.sec.gov/litigation/opinions.shtml.

name of the specific statute, or of one of the parties involved in the lawsuit, you need to use the appropriate finding aid tool.

When you start your search with a citation at hand, you need to interpret it. Figure 9 will provide you with the abbreviations for the federal repositories briefly discussed above, and identify each part of the abbreviation for a document contained in each of those repositories.

Any legal citation identifies a document as part of a print multi-volume legal collection. Thus, it is usually composed of three parts: a number that precedes the abbreviation, and which identifies the number of the volume of the collection, the abbreviation of the collection, and a number that follows the abbreviation and which identifies the page where the document starts. For example, if the citation you have is 78 Stat. 252, that means that you are looking for is a Public Law that is published in the 78th volume of the *Statutes at Large* and it starts on page 252.

Sometimes a citation will contain more than the three parts mentioned above. For example, the citation of a court's opinion contains the name of the parties, as well as the abbreviation of the reporter where it is published, which is preceded by the volume number and followed by the page where the opinion starts, and then by a parenthetical that contains the year when the case was decided. Those situations will be explained later, in the detailed discussion of how to find each type of legal document.

When you start your legal research without a citation, you need to fully use the information you have. For example, if you know the name of the statute and the number of the Congress that passed it, then it becomes manageable to locate it in the *Statutes at Large*. Each volume contains a list of the statutes it houses and it identifies them by their Public Law number and their name. For example, for the Civil Rights Act of 1964 you will go to the volumes of the 88th Congress, and browse through the lists. Thus, you will find out that the statute was published in the 78th volume and it starts on page 240.

Fig. 9
List of Abbreviations of Federal Primary Sources. Citing Federal Sources

1. Federal Statutes:
   a) *Statutes at Large*
      - Stat.
         - 78 Stat. 252 (Pub. L. No. 88-352)

           ↑ ↑ ↑
           vol. # abbr. pg #

   b) *United States Code*
      - U.S.C.
         - 42 U.S.C. § 2000d

           ↑ ↑ ↑
           title. # abbr. § number

2. Court Opinions. Supreme Court Opinions
   c) *United States Reports*
      - U.S.
         - Alexander v. Sandoval, 532 U.S. 275 (2001)

           ↑ ↑ ↑
           vol. # abbr. pg. #

3. Administrative Rules and Regulations
   a) *Federal Register*
      - Fed. Reg.
         - 65 Fed. Reg. 39775

           ↑ ↑ ↑
           vol. # abbr. pg #

   b) *Code of Federal Regulations*
      - C.F.R.
         - 34 C.F.R. § 100.1

           ↑ ↑ ↑
           title. # abbr. § number

If you want to read only a part of the Civil Rights Act of 1964 in its current version, then you should use the *United States Code* and its General Index. For example, if you want to read its Title VI, which focuses on the prevention of discrimination in federally assisted programs on racial grounds, then you go the General Index C-D, and search under the "civil rights" heading for "federal aid" and for "exclusion for participation . . . on grounds of race."[36] You will find that that statutory provision is codified in the 42nd title of the *United States Code* in Section 2000d. Of course, you can find the codified section by going to the electronic version of the *Code*, either directly to the GPO Access site,[37] or through FindLaw. You will follow the instructions from the *Code's* page that explain what type of Boolean search will more effective.

Similarly, when you do not have the citation of a case, but you know where the case was adjudicated and the names of the parties involved, then by choosing the appropriate court, within the limits explained below, you will be able to run a successful search in either LexisOne or FindLaw. The print reporters are multi-volume sets that do not have indexes that accompany each set. Without even a partial citation, which will identify the reporter and the volume where the opinion is published, you cannot locate it. Of course, almost all reporters have their own separate finding-aid tools that require special knowledge to use them. Those finding-aid tools are known as digests, and unless you search for older lower courts' cases, either LexisOne or Findlaw is a better place to search.

Both the *Federal Register* and the *Code of Federal Regulations* have finding-aid tools. So whether you know the citation of the document—65 Fed. Reg. 38775, or 34 C.F.R. Section 100.1—or only its subject matter, you should be able to locate it easily. Both the *Federal Register* and the *Code of Federal Regulations* can be accessed online either directly from the GPO Access Web site or from FindLaw.

---

36 UNITED STATES CODE (2000), General Index C-D, at 138.

37 *See* http://www.gpoaccess.gov/uscode/index.html.

Next we will talk about the two electronic services mentioned above: FindLaw and LexisOne. They are available free-of-charge from any corner of the world.

1. FindLaw: Electronic Portal to and Repository of Federal and State Law

FindLaw is an online service, a portal, or a legal Web site,[38] which is available at http://www.findlaw.com. It is both an online depository of law, because it provides legal resources on the Internet for both laymen and lawyers, and a portal to other online sources.

FindLaw[39] was started in 1995 by two attorneys as a list of Internet resources compiled for a workshop of the Northern California Law Librarians. Since then, both its content and its research capabilities have developed and currently it is part of the West legal publishing empire.

Currently, FindLaw provides more than the original list of Internet resources, which were already freely available online. An impressive portal to both federal and state law, FindLaw's list contains more than 50,000 human-edited legal site listings.

FindLaw lists two databases for federal legislation. It offers access to the *United States Code* in the version offered by the House of Representatives,[40] and in the version offered by Cornell's Legal Information Institute,[41] which is a mirror site of the government site. Additionally, FindLaw offers access to federal administrative

---

[38] For more information, *see* Company Background *at* http://company.findlaw.com/company_info.html.

[39] "FindLaw is the highest-trafficked legal Web site, providing the most comprehensive set of legal resources on the Internet for legal professionals, businesses, students and individuals. These resources include Web search utilities, cases and codes, legal news, [etc.]." *See* http://company.findlaw.com/.

[40] *See* the Office of the Law Revision Counsel, *at* http://uscode.house.gov/usc.htm.

[41] *See* http://www4.law.cornell.edu/uscode/.

law through both the *Federal Register* and the *Code of Federal Regulations* from their governmental Web sites at GPO Access.[42] FindLaw is a portal to state law as well. It directs you[43] to the official databases that each state's Web site hosts.

In addition to facilitating access to existing online sources FindLaw also provides access to its own legal electronic archive. FindLaw put together its own electronic depository of Supreme Court decisions that goes back to 1893. They are electronic copies of the decisions published in the official *United States Reports.* For example, the FindLaw text for Roe v. Wade, 410 U.S. 113 (1973), is that of the *United States Reports.* However, it does not include the *United States Reports'* pagination. Additionally, any opinion issued by the California Supreme Court and appellate court since 1934 is available from FindLaw with the pagination from the official state reporters.

2. LexisOne: Electronic Repository of and a Portal to Federal and State Law

Unlike FindLaw, which has joined forces with the West Group recently, LexisOne has always been the free online service of the other fee-based mega publisher LexisNexis.[44] LexisOne "a unique Web community" is available at http://www.lexisone.com.

LexisOne is the electronic database for federal and state (decisional) case law. It covers all the U.S. Supreme Court cases from 1790 to present and the last five years of published opinions from lower state and federal courts. Unlike the court opinions accessed from or through FindLaw, the LexisOne opinions contain the internal pagination of their corporate sponsor: LexisNexis.

---

42 *At* http://www.gpoaccess.gov/.

43 *See* http://www.findlaw.com/11stategov/indexconst.html.

44 "LexisONE® was launched in July 2000 by LexisNexis™." *See* http://www.lexisone.com/aboutlexisone/index.html.

LexisNexis™ is a member of Reed Elsevier PLC, which is owned equally by Reed International PLC (NYSE: RUK) and Elsevier NV (NYSE: ENL).

LexisOne also identifies the cases in its library through parallel citations to the official reporters, as well as to the commercial in-print reporter LexisNexis publishes. For example, the document we retrieve when we look for Miranda v. Arizona, 384 U.S. 436 (1966) has the internal LexisNexis pagination and it is identified with parallel citations from all the U.S. Supreme Court in-print reporters: the official *United States Reports*, and the two commercial ones, one that is published by West, *Suppreme Court Reporters* (abbreviated S. Ct.) and the other published by LexisNexis, *Lawyers' Edition* (abbreviated L. Ed.)

With respect to state law, LexisOne functions as a portal: it does not contain its own database. However, it offers a well-organized and well-represented access to the existing free databases.

H. COMPLETING YOUR RESEARCH

Finally, you have reached the last step of your legal research. You need to complete your research and make sure that your findings are still good law.

The big problem with legal research is related to the porous nature of law. Often in law, there is no clear answer. There is no rock to be located as in geology or a new insect to be described as in entomology. When do you know that what you have is the answer to your query? What represents the law? Is it a statute, a case, an administrative rule, or all of them? Is there a Supreme Court decision that has declared your findings unconstitutional? All these questions are pertinent, and, because of their intrinsic value, this book offers you a few research tips.

Start your research with a secondary source. Find a treatise, if there is one, or a law review article. When the answer is not there, arm yourself with the *Bluebook* and decipher the information you have. If there is a citation, read it correctly and learn the name of the repository where your document is collected.

Go to the appropriate repository in the appropriate format. If you need to read a statute in its original form, go to the *Statutes at*

Large. If you need to read the current version of a statutory provision, go to the *United States Code.*

If you need to read a case, go to either one of the electronic databases and portals identified above, keeping in mind their strengths and their limits. If you need to read an older case, whose subject matter is the only information you posses, then you need to restart your search and acquire more information, either about the court that issued it or the names of the parties. Then you may need to go to a library and learn how to use digests, the finding-aid tool that the West Publishing Company published to compliment its national collection of court reporters.

If you need to read an administrative rule or regulation, go to either the *Federal Register*, or the *Code of Federal Regulations* with the appropriate citation, or to the *Code of Federal Regulations* if you know only its subject matter and not the year when the regulation was issued. If you need an administrative decision, depending of how recent it is, you may consider going to the agency's Web site or locate it in a print reporter.

Of course, once you have located the legal norm of your interest, the question of its validity still applies. Has the Supreme Court held it unconstitutional? Has it been amended or reversed?

All these questions will be further addressed when we discuss researching the law in more detail. We will talk about updating each type of legal research—statutory, case law, and administrative—in those particular chapters. However, remember that this book focuses on legal research that is free-of-charge. American legal practitioners use either Lexis or Westlaw to update their legal research. Each commercial database has developed its own updating service: Lexis uses Shepard's and Westlaw uses KeyCite. For a fee, both services will reliably update the source whose citation you type in the appropriate search box in a matter of seconds.

Chapter 4
STATUTORY LAW: WHAT IT IS, WHERE IT IS, AND HOW YOU FIND IT

> Statutes are either general or special, public or private. A general or public act is an universal rule, that regards the whole community; and of this the courts of law are bound to take notice judicially without the statute being particularly pleaded.
>
> *Blackstone's The Study, Nature, and Extent of the Law*

A. INTRODUCTION

Often scholars start their introduction to American law with decisional law—court decisions—because, historically, courts have been the first resort for solving problems of civil cohabitation among people. "Courts are regularly open for the settlement of disputes, as legislatures are not."[1] But, today "decisional law [case law] stands below legislation in the hierarchy of authorities and case law is subject to change by statute."[2] Statues have binding authority over issues within their statutory subject matter, and courts must apply them to all disputes involving such issues. Furthermore, "legislation has so increased in quantity and importance in the United States during the past century"[3] that it only makes sense that we start our incursion in the study of legal rules with legislation.

Legislation—comprised of both federal and state statutes—is also known as statutory law. Through statutes legislative

---

1 Henry M. Hart, Jr. & Albert M. Sacks, *The Legal Process, Basic Problems, in* THE MAKING AND APPLICATION OF LAW 163 (1994).

2 E. ALLAN FARNSWORTH, AN INTRODUCTION TO THE LEGAL SYSTEM OF THE UNITED STATES 37 (3d ed. 1996).

3 *Id.* at 61.

bodies attempt to ensure social stability and make our future predictable.

Legislation represents a major component of legal regulation. Unlike case law—which is driven by particular controversies—it is the result of perceived public needs that requires a solution for the future. The source of statutory law is statutes and ordinances.

Statutes are the result of a legislative process that takes place at the federal, state, and even municipal level. The legislative process includes drafting bills and their passage through the legislative body and ends with the bill becoming a public or private law, a statute.

Once a statute governs a specific social activity, every time a dispute arises within that area of activity, courts will interpret the statute and solve the dispute according to the applicable statutory provision. In that process, the parties' attorneys will offer their own interpretation of the statute to the court, hoping that theirs will prevail. Interpreting statues, as further shown below, is a complex process, because often words do not translate into a single meaning.

In order to better understand how statutory law works, we will first briefly describe how statues are enacted and then identify the primary sources of statutory law: (a) the Constitution, (b–c) statutes enacted by Congress and the legislatures of the states, and (d) the ordinances issued by municipal bodies. Then we will talk about locating the appropriate repositories and a few basic techniques for finding specific statutory provisions. Finally we will talk about completing your research process and making sure that what you found is still good law.

B. THE LEGISLATIVE PROCESS AND ITS CONSTITUTIONAL BOUNDARIES

The U.S. Constitution defines the federal legislative body. Article 1, Section 1 states that "[a]ll legislative Powers herein granted shall be vested in a Congress of the United States, which shall consist of a Senate and House of Representatives."[4] In Article 1, Section

8 also identifies the areas—such as interstate commerce—over which Congress has legislative powers, and its enacted statutes are binding.[5] Additionally, Article I, Section 8 empowers Congress to "make all [other] Laws which shall be necessary and proper for carrying into Execution the foregoing Powers." This wording has caused many legal battles that often ended up in courts. As the result of such a legal battle, the Supreme Court may declare a federal statute unconstitutional. One such example was discussed earlier in the Supreme Court case of *United States v. Lopez*.[6]

In those areas, federal legislation takes precedence over conflicting state legislation; it is said that federal legislation preempts state legislation. For example, any "state cause of action securing to an author an exclusive right to copy a tangible expression clearly interferes with federal regulation [the Copyright Act] and is preempted."[7] The Copyright Act is codified in title 17 of the *United States Code*, and the preemption provisions are included in Section 301.

Similarly, at the state level, each state Constitution defines that state's legislative body. For example, Article III of the New York Constitution vests the state's power to pass statutes in a bi-cameral body made up of the Senate and Assembly.[8]

---

4 U.S. CONST. art. 1, § 1, in U.S.C.A. (2004).

5 U.S. CONST. art. 1, § 8, in U.S.C.A. (2004).

> The Congress shall have the Power To lay and collect Taxes, Duties, Imposts and Excises, to pay the Debts and provide for the common Defense and general Welfare of the United States; [. . .] .
>
> To make all Laws which shall be necessary and proper for carrying into Execution the foregoing Powers, and all other Powers vested by this Constitution in the Government of the United States, or in any Department or Office thereof.

6 514 U.S. 549 (1995).

7 ARTHUR MILLER & MICHAEL DAVIS, INTELLECTUAL PROPERTY. PATENTS, TRADEMARKS, AND COPYRIGHT, at 416 (2000).

8 N.Y. CONST. art III, §. 1 (McKinney 2001) ("The legislative power of this state shall be vested in the senate and assembly.").

C. THE LEGISLATIVE PROCESS. BRIEF REVIEW

Any federal statute starts as a bill.[9] Very few bills become statutes.

Passing a statute is not an easy process. It requires a lot of human energy and financial prowess to support the congressional members' interest in the statute. Sometimes the lobbying interests pushing for the passage of a bill are obvious; other times they are less obvious. For example, The Copyright Term Extension Act—Sonny Bono Copyright Term Extension Act[10]—extended the copyright term for works created on or after January 1, 1978, from life of the author plus 50 years after the author's death to life of the author plus 70 years after death. The act extended most other current copyrights for an additional 20 years.[11] The entertainment industry interests at work there are thus obvious. Other times those interests are not so clear.

Nevertheless, there are ways to speed a bill on its way or obstruct its advance to become a statute.[12] Some will become apparent from the discussion below. Also, there are ways to influence the ways in which a court will later apply a statute. Many of the records of legislative deliberations, which are often used to decipher statutory rules, should be regarded with suspicion when you interpret

---

9 Senate Bill S.1290 "To Amend Title 36 of the United States Code to establish the American Indian Education Foundation, and for Other Purposes." S. 1290 was introduced in the Senate on June 28, 1999. For the text of the bill as introduced in the Senate, *see* http://frwebgate.access.gpo.gov/cgi-bin/getdoc.cgi?dbname=106_cong_bills&docid=f:s1290is.txt.pdf. S.1290 was eventually voted and passed by Senate and then sent to the House for similar legislative action. For the text of the bill as passed by the Senate, *see* http://frwebgate.access.gpo.gov/cgi-bin/getdoc.cgi?dbname=106_cong_bills&docid=f:s1290es.txt.pdf.

10 Pub. L. No. 105-298, 112 Stat. 2817 (1998).

11 For a transcript of the Subcommittee on Courts and Intellectual Property's hearing dated June 27, 1997, go to http://commdocs.house.gov/committees/judiciary/hju43666.000/hju43666_0f.htm.

12 To see the summary of the legislative action taken by the Senate on bill S.1290, *see* http://thomas.loc.gov/cgi-bin/bdquery/z?d106:SN01290:–L&summ2=m&.

a statute, because they could have been inserted in the legislative record *post-factum* (after the debate itself) for the purpose of manipulating the reader's statutory interpretation.

As you all know the federal Congress is the body that makes federal statutes. Although, as mentioned before, its constitutional powers are limited, Congress is expected to legislate today on diverse issues, such as tariffs, public lands, currency, transportation, housing, education, foreign aid, and preemptive war. On the one hand, "[s]ources of ideas for legislation are unlimited."[13] On the other hand, Congress has a rigid procedure it follows to change those ideas into statutes. Of course, "proposed drafts of bills [may] originate in many diverse quarters."[14] Usually a member of Congress (representative or senator), will draft a bill and introduce it in one or both chambers of Congress. That member of Congress becomes the bill's sponsors. It is a senator for a bill introduced in the Senate and a representative for those introduced in the House of Representatives. For example, Senator Daniel Inouye introduced a bill to amend title 36 of the United States Code to establish the American Indian Education Foundation, on June 28, 1999, in the 106th Congress.[15] A related bill was introduced in the House, by representative Kildee on October 14, 1999.[16]

The *Index to the Congressional Record* of the Congress is the publication that keeps track of the action taken with every bill introduced. Thus, the *Index to the Congressional Record* of the first session

---

13 Charles W. Johnson, *How Our Laws Are Made*, H. Doc. 101–139 (2000), *available at* http://www.llpoh.org/HOW_OUR_LAWS_ARE_MADE.html.

14 *Id.*

15 *See* http://frwebgate.access.gpo.gov/cgi-bin/getdoc.cgi?dbname=106_cong_bills&docid=f:s1290is.txt.pdf.

16 House Bill H.R.3080 "To Amend the Indian Self-Determination and Education Assistance Act to Direct the Secretary of the Interior to Establish the American Indian Education Foundation, and for Other Purposes". H.R.3080 was introduced in the House on October 14, 1999. For the text of the bill as introduced in the House, *see* http://frwebgate.access.gpo.gov/cgi-bin/getdoc.cgi?dbname=106_cong_bills&docid=f:h3080ih.txt.pdf. For the summary of the legislative action taken by the House on H.R.3080, go to http://thomas.loc.gov/cgi-bin/bdquery/z?d106:HR03080:.

of the 106th Congress is the place to search for a summary of the actions taken on a bill.[17]

Most sponsors will insert an explanatory statement about their bills in the *Congressional Record* at some time on the day of introduction. Senator Daniel Inouye inserted his explanations,[18] and Representative Kildee, his.[19]

Once introduced, a bill is referred by the Speaker to the appropriate House standing committee for consideration and by the President Officer to the appropriate Senate committee. For example, the bill sponsored by Senator Daniel Inouye was referred to the Committee on Indian Affairs, and the bill sponsored by Representative Kildee was referred to the Committee on Resources.

After introduction and reference, all proposed bills are given a number and sent to the Government Printing Office. The next morning, printed copies are available in the Senate and House document rooms.

All bills have a designation. The bill introduced in the Senate will have the letter "S," which stands for Senate, followed by the bill number, while the bills introduced in the House will have "H.R.," which stands for House of Representatives, followed by the bill number. The Senate bill to amend title 36 of the United States Code was given the designation S. 1290,[20] while the House bill received the number H.R. 1380.[21]

---

17 This bill tracking service is available electronically for bills introduced within the last ten years, and it is a product of the Library of Congress. It is *available at* http://thomas.loc.gov/.

18 *See* http://frwebgate.access.gpo.gov/cgi-bin/getdoc.cgi?dbname=106_cong_bills&docid=f:s1290is.txt.pdf.

19 *See* http://frwebgate.access.gpo.gov/cgi-bin/getdoc.cgi?dbname=106_cong_bills&docid=f:h3080ih.txt.pdf.

20 *See* http://frwebgate.access.gpo.gov/cgi-bin/getdoc.cgi?dbname=106_cong_bills&docid=f:s1290is.txt.pdf.

21 *See* http://frwebgate.access.gpo.gov/cgi-bin/getdoc.cgi?dbname=106_cong_bills&docid=f:h3080ih.txt.pdf.

All bills have a title that succinctly states the subject or aim of the legislation. The short title of both the Senate bill S. 1290 and the House bill H.R. 1380 was the "American Indian Education Foundation Act of 1999."[22]

Most bills also contain a section that will explain the purpose of the bill, and another that will contain definitions of the terms they use. All bills contain standard clauses that will further detail the content of the bill.

For example, S. 1290 identifies its purpose in its title: "to establish the American Indian Education Foundation," whose own purpose is further itemized in Section 21602.[23] Similarly, H.R. 3080 identifies its purpose in its title and further details the scope of the American Indian Education Foundation in Section 501(e).[24]

The committee in charge of the future of a bill may hold hearings or may obstruct that process. When they hold hearings, that process ends with the committee writing a report that will accompany the bill when it is sent out to the Chamber's floor.

During those hearings, members of the Congress, as well as representatives of interest groups and other private persons may be heard. All those statements will become part of the "legislative history of the bill." At the committee level, there is considerable opportunity for delay and defeat of the bill. The Senate and Hose committee reports are published in a publication called the *United States Congressional Serial Set.*[25]

---

22 *See* S. 1290, *Summary and Status, at* http://thomas.loc.gov/cgi-bin/bdquery/D?d106:41:./temp/~bdAUZk:-L&summ2=m&.

23 S.1290 at 3, http://frwebgate.access.gpo.gov/cgi-bin/getdoc.cgi?dbname=106_cong_bills&docid=f:s1290is.txt.pdf.

24 H.R. 3080, at 2–3, http://frwebgate.access.gpo.gov/cgi-bin/getdoc.cgi?dbname=106_cong_bills&docid=f:h3080ih.txt.pdf.

25 Selected documents from the *Serial Set* volumes from 1833 to 1917 are available on the Library of Congress Web site, *at* http://memory.loc.gov/ammem/amlaw/lwsslink.html. For definitions of the documents available in the *Serial Set,* go to http://www.access.gpo.gov/su_docs/fdlp/history/sset/ssetbdef.html.

The Senate Committee on Indian Affairs held hearings on bill S. 1290, and published its report, as Senate Report 106-197.[26] Afterward the Senate unanimously voted on the bill and informed the House about its action.[27]

The House referred bill H.R. 3080 to the House Committee on the Judiciary. This committee further referred it to the Subcommittee on Immigration and Claims.[28] Not all bills are voted by a chamber as they are originally introduced in that chamber. For example, bill H.R. 3080 was voted in the House, but as part of another bill,[29] H.R. 5528, Omnibus Indian Advancement Act.[30]

A bill may be defeated on the floor of one of the chambers as well. For example, members of Congress may engage in making lengthy speeches intended to prevent or defeat action on the bill. This tactic is known as "filibustering," and it is recorded in a publication called the *Senate Journal*. While the *Senate Journal* is the official Senate publication, all Congressional floor proceedings are recorded—with noted inaccuracy—in a publication called the *Congressional Record*.

The *Congressional Record* is published daily while Congress is in session, and each daily edition has a digest that summarizes the floor and committees' activities for that day. However, both rep-

---

26 The final Senate Committee report on S.1290, the Report of the Senate Committee on Indian Affairs, Report 106-197, is *available at* http://frwebgate.access.gpo.gov/cgi-bin/getdoc.cgi?dbname=106_cong_reports&docid=f:sr197.106.pdf. For the final House Committee Report on HR. 3080, go to http://frwebgate.access.gpo.gov/cgi-bin/getdoc.cgi?dbname=106_cong_reports&docid=f:hr1028p1.106.pdf.

27 To see the summary of the legislative action taken by both chambers, go to http://thomas.loc.gov/cgi-bin/bdquery/z?d106:HR03080:–L&summ2=m& and http://thomas.loc.gov/cgi-bin/bdquerytr/z?d106:SN01290:.

28 *See* http://thomas.loc.gov/cgi-bin/bdquery/z?d106:SN01290:–C.

29 For the enrolled version of the H.R. 5528—as passed by the House, go to http://frwebgate.access.gpo.gov/cgi-bin/getdoc.cgi?dbname=106_cong_bills&docid=f:h5528eh.txt.pdf.

30 *Id.*

resentatives and senators interested in the bill's legislative history have been known to insert self-serving statements in the final version of the *Congressional Record*.[31] A separate volume is published for each calendar year.[32]

When a bill is approved in identical form by both the House and the Senate, the amendments are incorporated and the so-called "enrolled bill" is sent to the President for signature. The President has ten days in which to decide what action to take on the bill. The President may sign the bill or leave it unsigned and, if Congress is still in session, the bill becomes law in either case. However, the President may also refuse to sign the bill into law. The presidential refusal is called a "veto," and it may be overridden by a two-thirds vote of those present in both the Senate and the House—which has to be a quorum. If Congress overrides the veto, the bill becomes law.

Once the bill becomes law, it is transmitted to the General Services Administration for publication. When the bill is published it will be given a Public Law number (Pub. L. No.), which contains the number of the enacting Congress and a number indicating the order in which the bill was adopted as compared with other enactments by the same Congress.

The Omnibus Indian Advancement Act (the Act) was passed on December 27, 2000, and it became Public Law No. 106-568, or P.L. 106-568 (2000). Those numbers mean that the 106th Congress passed the Act as its 568th statute.

---

31 There are some stylistic differences between statements made at the time of the debate and those inserted later: bullets precede the Senate statements introduced later in the Record. *See* JANE GINSBURG, LEGAL METHODS: CASES AND MATERIALS, at 56 (2d ed. 2004).

32 The last ten volumes of the *Congressional Record* from 1990 (Vol. 140) through 2004 (Vol. 150) are available on the GPO Web site, *at* http://www.gpoaccess.gov/crecord/index.html. For definitions of the documents available in the *Serial Set*, go to http://www.access.gpo.gov/su_docs/fdlp/history/sset/ssetbdef.html.

The new law is published in its entirety with other new laws in a bound volume of the *Statutes at Large*, and it is also available online at the "United States Federal Legislative information service on the Internet," called Thomas[33] and on the Government Printing Office Web site.[34] The Omnibus Indian Advancement Act was published in volume 114 of the *Statutes at Large*, and it starts at page 2868. This Act may be identified by the location of the statute in the official publication as 114 Stat. 2868 (2000).

Thus, the original American Indian Education Foundation bill has become statute and gained binding authority upon all disputes involving related issues, as part of the Omnibus Indian Advancement Act, which is identified as Pub. L. No. 106-568, 114 Stat. 2868. The Omnibus Indian Advancement Act was incorporated in title 25 of the Code, which is called "Indians." The statute's codified version is identified as 25 U.S.C. Section 4101 et seq.[35]

D. IDENTIFYING THE SOURCES OF STATUTORY LAW

You now have a good idea of how statutes are enacted. Next let's identify all primary sources of statutory law. We include the Constitution as well.

1. The Constitution of the United States

If we were to view the American federal statutory system as a pyramid, then the Constitution of the United States will be its pinnacle. Furthermore, all legal rules of the land have to fit within the Constitution, as interpreted by the Supreme Court of the United States.

The Constitution is the highest law in our society because, although a very brief document, it spells out the structure of the federal government, and it regulates how our government works.

---

33 *See* http://thomas.loc.gov/.

34 *See* http://frwebgate.access.gpo.gov/cgi-bin/getdoc.cgi?dbname=106_cong_public_laws&docid=f:publ568.106.pdf.

35 *See* http://frwebgate3.access.gpo.gov/cgi-bin/waisgate.cgi?WAISdocID=82592911892+0+0+0&WAISaction=retrieve.

Chiefly, it sets out the norms that govern the distribution of political powers among the branches of government.

The U.S. Constitution, whose binding authority does not include the Declaration of Independence of July 4, 1776, is more recent than the Constitutions of many of the American states, which started being adopted as soon as we declared our independence from the British Empire. The federal Constitution was signed by the delegates to the Constitutional Convention in September 1787. Then it was submitted to the Continental Congress and became effective upon its ratification by two-thirds of the states, in July 1788.[36]

There were a few constitutional innovations presented in the federal Constitution that no other similar act has ever envisioned. Although the act itself is very short: only a few pages,[37] as we mentioned before, the Constitution delineates the structure of government. The first three articles identify the branches of the government: one for each branch, and enumerate each branch's duties.[38] In plain terms, it states that the federal government has limited powers. Article 1 of the Constitution limits the powers of the federal legislative body *vis-à-vis* the states of the Union.[39]

Although the principle of separation of powers was not new[40] it had not been previously embedded in a written Constitution. The Constitution does not mention whether one branch will have the

---

36 *See* THE CONSTITUTION OF THE UNITED STATES, 1 Stat. 10, *available at* http://memory.loc.gov/cgi-bin/ampage?collId=llsl&fileName=001/llsl001.db&recNum=133.

37 *See* CONSTITUTION OF THE UNITED STATES AND THE DECLARATION OF INDEPENDENCE, POCKET EDITION. (21st ed. 2003) (H. Doc. 108-96), *available at* http://frwebgate.access.gpo.gov/cgi-bin/getdoc.cgi?dbname=108_cong_documents&docid=f:hd096.pdf.

38 *Id.* at 1 et seq.

39 *Id.*

40 Montesquieu describes it in *The Spirit of the Law*, CHARLES DE SECONDAT, BARON DE MONTESQUIEU, THE SPIRIT OF LAWS (DE L'ESPIRIT DE LOIS) (G. Dublin, A. Ewing & G. Faulkner, 1751).

role of checking the use of power invested in the others.[41] However, because the principles of separation of powers was so scrupulously translated into separate articles describing the functions of each branch of the government, the check-and-balance function of the branches was easily assumed and, furthermore, the judiciary easily appointed itself the branch that checks the exercise of powers by the other branches.

Originally the Constitution contained only seven articles, with the last one dedicated to the ratification procedures.[42] Despite suggestions from various members to the 1787 Federal Convention in Philadelphia that the federal Constitution include a bill of rights that would secure some guarantees of personal liberty *vis-à-vis* the federal government, the Constitution did not include such a declaration of rights. Indeed, it mentioned some guarantees of what we consider today basic human rights—regarding access to courts and trial by jury[43]—but no Bill of Rights. However, the well-spread suspicion of the federal government prevailed and ten provisions—the Bill of Rights[44]—which empowered individuals against the power of the federal government, were soon added and sent to the states in 1789 to be ratified.[45]

---

41 CONSTITUTION OF THE UNITED STATES, *available at* http://frwebgate.access.gpo.gov/cgi-bin/getdoc.cgi?dbname=108_cong_documents&docid=f:hd096.pdf.

42 *Id.* at 16.

43 Art. III, § 2.

> Clause 3: The Trial of all Crimes, except in Cases of Impeachment, shall be by Jury; and such Trial shall be held in the State where the said Crimes shall have been committed; but when not committed within any State, the Trial shall be at such Place or Places as the Congress may by Law have directed.

Id. at 13.

44 *See* CONSTITUTION OF THE UNITED STATES, *available at* http://frwebgate.access.gpo.gov/cgi-bin/getdoc.cgi?dbname=108_cong_documents&docid=f:hd096.pdf.

45 CREATING THE BILL OF RIGHTS. THE DOCUMENTARY RECORD FROM THE

Aside from these first ten amendments, the Constitution has known 17 more amendments.[46] The 27th amendment became effective in 1992 and regards the compensation for services by senators and representatives.[47]

Thus, while initially it was mostly focused on the federal government and its powers *vis-à-vis* the states and the individuals—by incorporating the Bill of Rights—and after the adoption of the Reconstruction Era Amendments, 13th, 14th, and 15th Amendments in the years following the Civil War, the Constitution has become our main guarantor of individual freedoms and liberties. It imposes limits on both the federal and the state governments. For example, the Fourth Amendment guarantees our freedom from unwarranted searches and seizures, protecting us from unreasonable intrusion by both the federal and state governments.

While the Constitution is the repository of our main individual freedoms, the U.S. Supreme Court is the institution that gives meaning to those rights by making sure that no statute or administrative rule violates our fundamental law. The judicial branch is thus the ultimate arbiter of constitutionality. In other words, it can be argued that it is not the Constitution itself, but the Supreme Court's interpretation of it that establishes the standard of legality in our system.

2. Federal Statutes

Article I, Section 1 of the Constitution of the United States identifies the federal legislative body and states that "all legislative Powers herein granted shall be vested in a Congress of the United States." If Article I empowers Congress to pass statutes, which are the source of legislation, Article VI, paragraph 2, of the Constitution establishes the that federal legislation occupies the next

---

FIRST FEDERAL CONGRESS (Helen E. Veit, Kenneth R. Bowling & Charlene Bangs Bickford eds., 1991).

46 *Id.* at 23–34.

47 *Id.* at 34.

place in the hierarchy of our legal system, next to the Constitution itself. This article is usually referred to as the "supremacy clause:"

> This Constitution, and the Laws of the United States which shall be made in Pursuance thereof; and all the Treaties made, or which shall be made, under the Authority of the United States, shall be the supreme Law of the Land; and the Judges in every State shall be bound thereby, any Thing in the Constitution or Laws of any State to the Contrary notwithstanding.

Federal statutory law is not formally limited to domestic statutes. It also includes treaties concluded with other countries. In our system, any foreign treaty to which the Untied States is a party is not automatically binding. Congress must approve it, through the process of ratification that ends with Congress incorporating the treaty into a domestic statute.

3. State Statutes

Every state has its own Constitution. Unlike the federal Constitution, state Constitutions contain many specific rules for diverse activities such as school, police administration, or state and municipal budgeting.

Those Constitutions, exactly like the federal one, identify each state's legislative body and its prerogatives. The state legislative bodies will enact state statutes. Unlike federal statutes, the state statutes will have a limited geographical application, and, of course, will govern different social activities. Those statues are subject to challenge in state courts on state constitutional grounds and in federal courts on federal grounds. For example, issues related to obtaining your driver's license will be tried in state courts. On the other hand, issues related to the constitutionality of such procedures will be tried in federal courts.

4. Municipal Ordinances

Each municipal unit has its own charter—fundamental law—and, of course, its own legislative branch. The municipal legislative bodies enact rules that deal with diverse issues of local importance: collecting the garbage, parking fines, or noise. Such rules of local legislative origin are commonly called "ordinances." These local lawmaking bodies are not considered part of the legislative branch in other countries. In France, for example, as in many other countries that follow the civil law system, they are part of the administrative branch.

New York City's legislative branch is called the City Council. The New York City Council enacts local laws.[48]

If these are the diverse sources of legislation, next let's see how these sources are created. Let's see how the legislative process works and how statues are made at the federal level.

E. APPLYING LEGISLATION: INTERPRETING STATUTES

Once enacted, statutory provisions are binding on all activities that come within their boundaries. In case of a dispute, courts are required to follow the statutory provisions. For example, when a former employee sued the Bureau of Indian Affairs alleging wrongful termination of his employment, the court had to apply the applicable statutory provision. In *Bear Robe v. Parker*[49] the court applied the "Indian Child Protection and Family Violence Prevention Act"—as amended on December 27, 2000, by the Omnibus Indian Advancement Act of 2000[50]—which stated that the employee's previous conviction for voluntary manslaughter was an absolute bar to employment in a position that involved regular contact with Indian children. The Act did not say anything about the potential mitigating factor of the employee's "successful employment at the school."[51] However, the court ruled that the

---

48 The most recent New York City local laws can be accessed online, *at* http://www.nyccouncil.info/issues/index.cfm.

49 270 F.3d 1192 (8th Cir. 2001).

50 Pub. L. No. 106-568, § 814, 114 Stat. 2868, 2918 (2000).

51 270 F.3d at 1194.

previous conviction constituted an absolute bar to employment, and explained its ruling stating that

> Congress has adopted a bright line rule that persons who fall within the Act's proscriptions are not to be employed in positions that involve regular contact with children in federally funded Indian schools.[52]

Despite the fact that the Eighth Circuit Court of Appeals decided in this case that the statutory language was clear, a different interpretation of the provision is not far fetched. In fact the plaintiff in *Bear Robe* started his lawsuit because he (or his attorney) did not think that the statutory provision was crystal clear. How is this ambiguity possible?

In order to apply a statute to a specific factual situation, courts read the statutory provision, interpret it, and apply it accordingly. But there is no clear understanding about how statutes should be interpreted.

"The interpretative status quo is cacophonous. Every judge and scholar has his own theory of how best to interpret statutes, and this diversity renders the interpretative project unpredictable."[53]

However, that said, there are a few rules that may guide the process of interpreting statutes. Three of them will be briefly explained below.

1. The "Plain Meaning Rule"

As its title suggests, the gist of this rule is that "the words alone suffice." This rule rejects the need to look beyond the words of the statute as passed by Congress. It rejects the need to look at the records created during the passage of the bill in the legislature—

52 *Id.* at 1195.

53 Nicholas Quinn Rosenkrantz, *Federal Rules of Statutory Interpretation*, 115 HARV. L. REV. 2085, 2088 (2002).

to what is known as the legislative history of the bill—in order to ascertain what the legislature "intended."

This rule is sometimes mentioned by state statutes. For example, according to the New York statutes: "Where words of a statute are free from ambiguity and express plainly and clearly and distinctly the legislative intent, resort may not be had to other means of interpretation."[54] Sometimes, courts adopt it and incorporate it in their decisions, holding that that "the act is clear upon its face."[55]

However, this rule of interpretation has an obvious weakness: words have rarely one meaning; they are hardly ever transparent. Words rarely say what they mean. "A word is not a crystal, transparent and unchanged," Justice Holmes rightly observed "it is the skin of a living thought and may vary greatly in color and content according to the circumstances and the time win which it is used."[56]

2. Interpreting Statutes in Light of Their Legislative History

Another guiding rule for interpreting statutes is by using the record created during the legislative process when the statute was born. Formally speaking, there is a difference between inquiry into the language of a statute and inquiry into the legislature's intent. The goal remains the same: what does this statute say? The approach is different.

The proponents of this rule believe that because words are imperfect symbols of communication, the most accurate way of determining the meaning of legislation is finding the preexisting understanding of its legislators regarding specific issues covered in the legislation. They believe that the records that trail the legislative process contain that preexisting understanding, and they access the records according to their probative value.

---

54 N.Y. STAT. LAW § 76. *See also* §§ 71–424.

55 Brown J., in Hamilton v. Rathbone, 175 U.S. 414 (1899).

56 Towne v. Eisner, 245 U.S. 418, 425 (1918).

It is commonly accepted that the legislative committee reports are of greatest importance, because they contain written assessments of the legislation by members of Congress that have studied it, heard testimony and arguments for and against it, and eventually voted to send it to the floor for a vote. Of a value equal to committee reports are statements of individual legislators responsible for the preparation or drafting of the bill.

Statements in debates on the floor of Congress are considered less persuasive, because they can be inserted in the legislative record at a later time. Among the Supreme Court Justices, Justice Scalia is the strongest opponent of the use of legislative history in interpreting statutes. Instead Justice Scalia favors the "plain meaning rule" in its "originalist" version. Rightfully so, Justice Scalia opposes using statements of individual legislators, because they are ordinarily addressed to a virtually empty room or concocted to influence courts, which are later called on to interpret the statute.[57] However, he relies on the "originalist" fiction that today we can and we should interpret concepts within the meaning they had at the time they became legislation.[58]

The problem with the legislative history approach is often a misunderstanding of the role of "legislative purpose." Of course, legislators had a purpose when they passed a specific piece of legislation. That purpose is to govern a specific social interaction for the future. Of course, that purpose may be transparent if we read the records of the statute's legislative history. But if we are to interpret the statute for the future and not for the past, we have to accept that our interpretation is appropriately flawed. If the statute is still needed, it is because it can answer present needs, and those needs could not have been answered at a time when,

---

[57] *See* Crosby v. National Foreign Trade Council, 530 U.S. 363, 391 (2000) (Scalia, J., concurring) and Blanchard v. Bergeron, 489 U.S. 87, 98–99 (1989).

[58] R. Randall Kelso, *The Natural Law Tradition on the Modern Supreme Court: Not Burke, But the Enlightenment Tradition Represented by Locke, Madison, and Marshall*, 26 St. Mary's L.J. 1051, 1058–59 (1994–1995).

perhaps, they did not exist. In other words, if we cannot make sense of a statute's meaning in the social, economic, and political context of the present, past explanations will only encumber our process instead of helping it. For example, due process of law meant one thing to the Founding Fathers—it clearly did not encompass women and African-Americans—and another thing to today's Supreme Court justices—who have determined that substantial due process prohibits qualifying anal sex between same sex partners as deviate sex as long as identical sexual practices between heterosexuals are not considered "deviate."[59] Even if we were to go back and read everything that can illuminate our understanding of the Founding Father's own understanding, reality is that whatever the Supreme Court justices decide today, will govern the meaning of due process of law today.

Finally, the records of legislative history are documents that ultimately are read today with today's understanding, and the entire exercise of going back in time and pretending that we apply some legislators' intent to deciphering those documents and not our own understanding seems to be nothing more than mere legal fictions necessary to legitimize the ultimate result.

3. The Purposive Analysis: The "Social Purpose" Rule

Under the "social purpose" rule, a statute will be construed to accomplish the social purpose it was designed to accomplish. A version of the social purpose rule is the "absurdity" limit on the plain meaning rule. For example, in *Green v. Bock Laundry*,[60] the Supreme Court declined to read the Federal Rule of Evidence literally, partly because a literal reading would have made unintended absurd distinctions. A literal reading of the word "defendant" in Federal Rule of Evidence 609(a) would have meant that in a civil case, evidence of a prior criminal conviction could be introduced to attack the credibility of the *defendant* but not that

---

59 Lawrence v. Texas, 539 U. S. 558 (2003).

60 490 U.S. 504 (1989).

of the plaintiff. The Court found that distinction irrational. The Court thus gave priority to a reading that emphasized the purpose of the legislation.

Although not identified as such, for example, the rule of interpretation favored by Justice Ginsburg during her confirmation hearing emphasized the fact that the meaning of constitutional concepts needs to and does evolve over time. For example, during her confirmation hearing,[61] Justice Ginsburg pointed out the absurdity of refusing such an approach when courts interpret the general concept of equality. The concept can be found in the Declaration of Independence, as well as in the 14th Amendment. At none of those times did either the Founding Fathers or the Framers of the Equal Protection Clause of the 14th Amendment have equal rights for women specifically in mind. However, today such a historically correct interpretation seems clearly absurd.

To a large extent, all statutory provisions are bound to be interpreted by courts following the rules briefly detailed above. Next let's identify the repositories of statutory law.

F. REPOSITORIES OF STATUTORY LAW

1. The Constitution of the United States

The Constitution is available both in print and electronically free-of-charge. It is also accessible through the two official statutory compilations: *Statutes at Large* and the *United States Code*, both in print and online. The mimeographed collection of historic Statutes at Large, and thus the Constitution, is available through the Library of Congress's Web site, *A Century of Lawmaking for a New Nation: U.S. Congressional Documents and Debates, 1774–1875*.[62] The most recent

---

61 *The Supreme Court: Excerpts from Senate Hearings on the Ginsburg Nominations* N.Y. TIMES: July 21, 1993, at 12. For a general commentary, *see also* R. Randall Kelso, *The Natural Law Tradition on the Modern Supreme Court: Not Burke, But the Enlightenment Tradition Represented by Locke, Madison, and Marshall*, 26 ST. MARY'S L.J. 1051, 1069–70 (1994–1995).

62 *Available at* http://memory.loc.gov/cgi-bin/ampage?collId=llsl&fileName=001/llsl001.db&recNum=133

version of the Constitution is available electronically, as part of the *United States Code,* from the full-text database offered by GPO Access, a service of the U.S. Government Printing Office.[63]

Additionally, the Constitution is also available from the commercial federal statutory databases, both in print and electronically. They will be further discussed below.

2. Federal Statutes

Both state and federal legislation are published in two ways: chronologically and topically. The chronological publication is called, at the federal level, *Statutes at Large.*[64]

Statutes at Large contains the laws passed by Congress, and each volume has a table of contents that lists the laws passed by that Congress in that specific session by their title and their public or private number.[65] Additionally, the general and permanent laws of the United States are also published in a multi-volume collection that is organized by subject matter, according to 50 numbered titles that cover broad areas, such as "Hospitals and Asylums" (title 24) or "War and National Defense" (title 50). This codified version is called the *United States Code.* As mentioned before the *Statutes at Large* and the *United States Code* are the official statutory collections because they are published by the government. They are both available in print and electronically.

In addition, the codified version of the federal statutes is also published in two commercial publications: the West Group and

---

63 *See* http://www.gpoaccess.gov/uscode/index.html.

64 The first 18 volumes of the *Statutes at Large*—from 1789 through 1875—are available on the Library of Congress's Web site, *at* http://memory.loc.gov/ammem/amlaw/lwsllink.html.

65 Public and private laws are prepared and published by the Office of the Federal Register (OFR), National Archives and Records Administration (NARA). *GP Access* contains the text of public and private laws enacted from the 104th Congress to the present. They can be accessed *at* http://www.gpoaccess.gov/plaws/. The Library of Congress also houses Public Laws from the 93rd Congress onward, *at* http://thomas.loc.gov/.

LexisNexis. The West product is called the *United States Code Annotated* and the Lexis product is called the *United States Code Service*. The *United States Code* is abbreviated U.S.C., the *United States Code Annotated* is abbreviated U.S.C.A., and the *United States Code Service* is abbreviated U.S.C.S. Thus, you may see references to 42 U.S.C. Section 2000d as 42 U.S.C.A. Section 2000d or 42 U.S.C.S. Section 2000d. They will contain the same statutory provision. The only difference is that the commercial publications have editorial enhancements: annotations that provide reference to cases and administrative rules, for example. Of course, the information provided in annotations, cases, and administrative rules and decisions, is included in some free legal databases, but it is harder to find there.

3. State Statutes

Like the federal statutes, state statutes are published both chronologically and topically, in Codes. At the state level, the chronological publication of legislation carries different names from *North Carolina Session Laws*, to *Laws of Illinois*, or *Kentucky Acts*. Usually, each state has one official publication of session laws and one or more commercial publications. The most current edition of the official publication of session laws is usually available from the state legislature's Web site free-of charge.[66] The commercial publications are usually available from the commercial service that is associated with the publishing company, either Westlaw or Lexis.

For example, the official version of session laws for the state of New York is called, *Laws of New York*. The commercial publications are *McKinney's Session Laws of New York*, published by West, and available from Westlaw, and *New York Consolidated Laws Service Session Laws*, published by Lexis, and available from Lexis.

---

66 The current *North Carolina Session Laws* are available on the state legislature's Web site, *at* http://www.ncleg.net/statutes/statutes.asp. The *Laws of Illinois* are available on the state legislature's Web site, *at* http://www.legis.state.il.us/legislation/publicacts/default.asp. Similarly, *Kentucky Acts* are available on the state legislature's Web site, *at* http://lrc.ky.gov/acts/main-acts.htm.

While the federal code is published both by governmental and by private publishers, the state codes are usually published only by private publishers. For example, while the New York statutes used to be published in an official statutory compilation called *The Consolidated Laws of New York*, currently, there is no official codification in print.[67] However the consolidated laws of New York are available from the state legislature's Web site.[68] Some state codes are published by both major legal publishers, West and Lexis. For example, Kentucky has two codifications: *Baldwin's Kentucky Revised Statutes Annotated* is published by West, while *Michie—Kentucky Revised Statutes Annotated* is published by Lexis. Some states, like New York, have three commercial codified versions of the consolidated laws: *McKinney's Consolidated Laws of New York Annotated*, published by West and available on Westlaw, *New York Consolidated Laws Service*, published by Lexis and available on Lexis, and *Gould's Consolidated Laws of New York*, published by Gould Publications.

4. Municipal Ordinances

Each municipal unit has its own charter—fundamental law—and, of course, its own legislative branch. New York City's legislative branch is called the City Council, and it predecessor was the Common Council.[69] The City Council enacts local laws in annual council sessions. Although, often, there are no published session laws similar to the state collection, the municipal local laws are available both in print and electronically.[70] The New York City local laws are published in the *New York City Legislative Annual.*

As you can see, there are diverse sources of legislation. Each type of legislation has its own repository. For doing effective research you need to understand what you need as early as possi-

---

67 ELLEN GIBSON, NEW YORK LEGAL RESEARCH GUIDE I-68 (2d ed. 1998).

68 *See* http://assembly.state.ny.us/leg/?sl=0.

69 ELLEN GIBSON, NEW YORK LEGAL RESEARCH GUIDE II-6 (2d ed. 1998).

70 The most recent New York City local laws can be accessed online *at* http://www.nyccouncil.info/issues/index.cfm.

ble. That is why using a secondary source is vital to your enterprise. Once you identify the appropriate legal repository, you need to locate a specific statutory provision within it.

G. HOW TO LOCATE SPECIFIC PRIMARY SOURCES OF STATUTORY LAW

Once you have identified the primary source of statutory law, you need to make further use of the information you had when you started your research. You need to locate the specific statutory provision within the rather impressive repositories of statutory law.

If you start your research with a citation, make sure that you have a copy of the *Bluebook* handy in order to avoid wild goose chases. For example, if your citation reads N.Y.C.R.R., do not think that the abbreviation is that of a collection of New York City rules and regulation. Use the Bluebook and learn its correct meaning, that of the *New York Code of Rules and Regulations.* Once you deciphered the citation, check a library catalog for the collection whose title is abbreviated in the citation, and find what you need remembering that the number preceding the abbreviation indicates the number of the volume or the title and the number that follows the abbreviation indicates the section or the page within the volume or title. For example, a citation to a session laws collection will contain the number of the volume, the abbreviation, and the number of the page where the statute starts, while a citation to a codified statutory compilation will contain the number of the title containing the provision, the abbreviation of the compilation, and the number of the section of the statutory provision within that title. (See Chapter 3, Fig. 9.)

When you start your research with a topic, then you should go to the codified version of the statutory compilation. For example, if you want to search for the copyright preemption provision, go to the print Index to the *United States Code,* or to the electronic version of the *United States Code,* which is available from the legal portal FindLaw.[71] If you choose FindLaw, click on the tab "Searching Cases and Codes." Once there, choose the link that directs you to the U.S. Code. Once you have made the choice of your database, type "copyright preemption" in the keyword search box. If you know the citation, type 17 U.S.C. Section 301 in the appropriate search boxes. Please note that while the *United States Code* is available online at the GPO Access site in its 2000 version (which is the edition of its print publication), on FindLaw your result is dated 2002.

At the same time, remember that all Public Laws are available through fee-based databases, and both Lexis and Westlaw cover the *United States Code.* Additionally, both Lexis and Westlaw allow you to browse the *Code's* table of contents. Moreover, Westlaw gives you the option to use online either the *Index to the United States Code Annotated* or the *USCA Popular Name Table,* which, unlike the *Index,* lists statutes by their names.

Similarly, if you want to search state law, and if know the citation to one of the statutory compilations, translate it into its full title by using the *Bluebook.* Then find the compilation in a library collection. If you know the topic, use the *Index* to the codified compilation, or you may try to do a search on one of the free online databases. However, if you have access to either Lexis or Westlaw, remember that both cover state statutory law, and a keyword search in their full-text libraries will be more likely to produce relevant results.

With municipal law your search may be trickier, as the primary sources are more obscure. However, remember that there often is a published index for municipal law in your local public library and that recent municipal ordinances are searchable online. An annual index of the New York local laws is located in the *New York City Legislative Annual.* Similarly, both Lexis and Westlaw cover municipal law, and a search using those databases, though expensive, will have the same virtues exposed so many times here.

---

71 *See* http://www.findlaw.com/.

H. COMPLETING YOUR RESEARCH: THE U.S. LEGAL SYSTEM—A SYSTEM OF EVER-EVOLVING STATUTORY LAW

The U.S. legal system consists of norms that continue to adapt to social-economic changes and, of course, to our ever-changing mores. When the source of those norms is statutory, it is your final research step to make sure that that statute is still good law. A statute is still good law when it is still binding authority over the area it is supposed to regulate.

Statutes may fall into desuetude. The activities they are called upon to regulate either disappear or become normal, when once considered deviant, and there is no desire to enforce the statute. For example, changes in mores change the way statutes are enforced. While adultery[72] is still a crime (although not a capital one anymore[73]), rarely is one prosecuted for it.[74]

Statutes and their rules may sometime be declared unconstitutional. Some may take decades to be held unconstitutional; others may be declared as such within a few years. The Racial Integrity Act of 1924 little by little fell in desuetude, but when the Supreme Court finally declared it unconstitutional in 1966, *Loving v. Virginia*,[75] there still were 16 states in which interracial marriage continued to be illegal.

---

[72] Adultery means sexual intercourse between consenting adults during a time when at least one of the partners is married to someone else. Adultery is distinguished from fornication, which is sexual intercourse between unmarried, consenting adults.

[73] Dana Neacşu, *Tempest in a Teacup or the Mystique of Sexual Legal Discourse*, 38 GONZ. L. REV. 601 613 (2002/03) ("the Puritans of the Massachusetts Bay Colony used laws to punish extra-marital sex and they chose to do so by defining adultery as a capital crime. It should be noted that people remained undeterred despite such a threat.").

[74] For a well-publicized case of adultery, that of Lt. Kelly Flinn, *see, e.g.*, James M. Winner, Capt, USAF, *Beds with Sheets but No Covers: The Right to Privacy and the Military's Regulation of Adultery*, 31 LOYOLA L.A. L. REV. 1073 (1998).

[75] 388 U.S. 1 (1967).

In *Griswold v. Connecticut*,[76] the Supreme Court declared unconstitutional Connecticut criminal statutes that had been revised only a few years previously. The 1958 revision criminalized the activity defined as "preventing conception."[77]

In *Griswold* the Court found the 1958 revision unconstitutional[78] on grounds that it violated "several fundamental constitutional guarantees" that the Court defined as one's "zone of privacy" or "area of protected freedoms."[79] The Connecticut statute was repealed (never applied) after the Court decision.

The Connecticut statute reflected Connecticut's sense of social order and reproductive interests as existed in the 1950s. The Supreme Court decision clearly mirrored a different sense of order, at the national level. Indirectly, the Court decision deemed the Connecticut statute unable to reflect the social needs of the present; it was thus inappropriate for its role of governing Connecticut reproductive relationships within the realm of marriage for the future.

With *Griswold*, the Supreme Court legitimized the needs of a segment of the population of the United States that was becoming more and more active on the political arena: middle-class women. With that decision, the Court further established its role in the cultural war that still continues between the social liberals and the social conservatives,[80] and, of course, its role of defining

---

76 381 U.S. 479 (1965).

77 CONN. GEN. STAT. § 53–32 (1958). This provision was added to those of attempting miscarriage or encouraging the commission of abortion. CONN. GEN. STAT. § 7–1155 (1902); CONN. GEN. STAT. § 7–1157 (1902).

78 CONN. GEN. STAT. § 53–32 (1958).

> Any person who uses any drug, medicinal article or instrument for the purpose of preventing conception shall be fined not less than fifty dollars or imprisoned not less than sixty days nor more than one year or by both fined and imprisoned.

79 381 U.S. at 486.

80 For a more detailed discussion about social liberal and social conser-

our social order. Of course, there are other decisions that marked our present history equally dramatically. For example, *Brown v. Board of Education* (I)[81] and the opinion mentioned above in *Loving v. Virginia.*[82]

The U.S. Supreme Court is our main institution of checks and balances, and no statute is safe from constitutional review even when it has been examined once. For example, twice the Court focused on the Child Online Protection Act.[83] This act sought to protect children from exposure to commercial pornography placed on the Internet. See *Ashcroft v. American Civil Liberties Union.*[84]

That being said, each statutory search needs to end with updating your research. You need to check whether the statute has been amended or whether the Supreme Court has declared it unconstitutional.

If the codified version of you statute predates 2000, then you need to check it in the most recent version of the federal Code, the 2000 edition, and then further follow the steps delineated here. If your statutory provision comes from the most recent version of the federal Code, then all you need to do is to update your results through a search in the electronic database that covers *Statutes at Large* Similarly, if your search brought up a statue enacted since the last codification, you will update your search using *Statutes at Large.* Such a search can be done through the free-of-charge governmental databases. You should abandon the cita-

---

vative agendas and how they are furthered today, *see, e.g.*, Dana Neacşu, *Tempest in a Teacup or the Mystique of Sexual Legal Discourse,* 38 GONZ. L. REV. 601 (2003/2003).

81 347 U.S. 483 (1954) available both through FindLaw, *at* http://caselaw.lp.findlaw.com and through LexisOne at http://www.lexisone.com.

82 388 U.S. 1 (1967) available both through FindLaw, *at* http://caselaw.lp.findlaw.com and through LexisOne, *at* http://www.lexisone.com.

83 47 U.S.C. § 231.

84 124 S. Ct. 2783 (2004) available both through FindLaw, *at* http://caselaw.lp.findlaw.com and through LexisOne at http://www.lexisone.com.

tion and perform this last segment of your search focusing on the topic of your statute.

Once you updated your statutory results, you need to make sure that there are no court decisions holding that statutory provision unconstitutional. We will detail those steps in Chapter 5.

Of course, if you have access to either Lexis or Westlaw, as mentioned above, all you need to do is to use their updating service, Shepard's or KeyCite. Each service allows you to update your results by typing the legal citation for the primary source in which you are interested. The results will vary according to the statutory importance of you result. However, they will cover statutes, case law, and administrative rules and regulations.

In the next chapter we will focus on decisional law. It will talk about the ways in which judges make law, the ways in which you can discern what part of an opinion contains the legal ruling, and how decisions become law through the principle of *stare decisis.* It will also talk about decisional law research and the ways in which you can update it.

Chapter 5
CASE LAW: WHAT IT IS, WHERE IT IS, AND HOW YOU FIND IT

> [. . .] to accomplish the redress of [. . .] injuries, courts of justice are instituted in every civilized society, in order to protect the weak for the insults of the stronger, by expounding and enforcing those laws, by which rights are defined and wrongs prohibited. This remedy is therefore principally to be sought by application to these courts of justice that is, by civil suit or action.
>
> The doctrine of the law then is this: that precedents and rules must be followed, unless flatly absurd or unjust: for though their reason be not obvious at first view, yet we owe such a deference to former times as not to suppose they acted wholly without consideration. Upon the whole, however, we may take it as a general rule, "that the decisions of courts of justice are the evidence of what is common law."
>
> *Blackstone's The Study, Nature, and Extent of the Law*

A. COURT OPINIONS: THE END RESULT OF A LAWSUIT

Court opinions are the primary source of decisional (case) law. If a court is "the place wherein justice is judicially administered,"[1] a court opinion is the place where you can locate that justice.

A court opinion is always the end product of a process—a lawsuit—that varies in complexity. Although an opinion is not pre-

[1] EHRLICH'S BLACKSTONE, at 465 (1959).

ceded by the effort the passing of a statute requires, in its own way it demands a lot of both human and financial resources.

Like the majority of our daily activities, which are governed by rules, legal disputes also are governed by rules. As you know, there are rules that state our rights and duties and disclose the circumstances in which a court may be expected "to grant redress to one person against another."[2] The rules that state our rights and duties are considered rules of substance and make the body of substantive law. There are also rules that govern the process of enforcing substantive rules, when those are violated.

Those rules are usually considered to be procedural in their nature. For example, a substantive rule states that A has the right to lawful employment and that if A is denied such employment, A is entitle to a judgment of a court to recover money damages from B. The procedural rule will state what A has to do in order to recover the money damages from B. Such procedural rules make the body of civil procedure, or civil litigation. In other words, procedural law prescribes "the procedures by which persons may bring disputes before courts"[3] and by which they unfold.

The stages civil litigation usually follows are briefly described below.

1. The Pleading Stage

When people have a dispute, they usually go to a lawyer who will change it into a lawsuit. Of course, people may start lawsuits without the help of a lawyer. Then they become *pro se* litigants.

Upon listening to the facts, lawyers may decide to represent the prospective client. In exchange for legal representation, lawyers usually charge their clients an hourly wage. Sometimes they may accept a contingency fee representation and the client will not incur any pecuniary loss because the attorney is paid a percentage

---

[2] RICHARD H. FIELD ET AL., CIVIL PROCEDURE: MATERIALS FOR A BASIC COURSE at 3 (8th ed. 2003).

[3] *Id.* at 4.

of the damages won in the case. Very rarely, lawyers represent clients on a *pro bono* basis and do not incur any pecuniary gain for their services.

The document that starts a civil action is a complaint, and it contains causes of action that explain the legal grounds for the action. When a private wrong—infringement of an individual's right—is sought to be remedied, a civil action is started. On the contrary, when a public wrong—a violation of the pubic rights and duties due to the whole community—is sought to be corrected, the state will commence a criminal case. Unlike a civil case, a criminal case often attempts to secure obedience to the state's laws through the physical punishment of the lawbreaker.[4]

The party who starts the lawsuit is called the plaintiff. The party against whom a remedy is sought will become the defendant. The remedy sought in a civil action is usually a pecuniary one—the payment of money. In addition to damages—request for a money payment—the plaintiff may also seek equitable relief. Seeking equitable relief is asking the court to issue an injunction that will order the defendant to do or not to do something.

Once the complaint is filed, the alleged wrongdoer—the defendant—is informed about the legal action taken against it. The defendant will be served with the necessary legal papers that will offer support for building a defense.

2. The Discovery Stage

When the pleading stage is over, the more time consuming phase of a civil trial starts. This is the discovery stage, and it follows procedural rules according to the court where the litigation started: state or federal. The basic purpose of the federal rules regarding discovery remains to ensure that the parties to civil litigation "could obtain disclosure of all relevant information in the possession of any person before trial, unless the information was privileged."[5]

---

4 *Id.* at 2.

5 Larry Teply & Ralph Whitten, Civil Procedure, at 740 (2d ed. 2000).

The amount of discovery in civil cases depends on the parties' financial prowess. Discovery means labor hours for attorneys. During this stage, lawyers for both parties will try to discover facts that will substantiate their clients' allegations—of injury, for the plaintiff, and of non-feasance for the defendant.

An easy scenario is the one in which the defendant answers with strong counterclaims and moves to have the court dismiss the plaintiff's case for failure to state a cause of action. Such a strong reaction may intimidate the plaintiff and induce it to tell its attorney that it does not want to prosecute the case any longer. That often ends the case with an out-of-court settlement.

But, usually, discovery is a process that takes months because each party's attorneys try to procure proof for their clients' allegations. Discovery means gathering the information needed to build a winning case in court. It involves discovery requests by asking the other party to provide as much information as possible through a large array of documents. Those documents have specific names and their use during the pretrial stage is strictly regulated by procedural rules. For example, the Rules of Federal Procedure—Federal Rule of Civil Procedure 26—require that all disclosures, requests for discovery, and responses to discovery requests be signed by the party's attorney.

Among the most popular discovery means are "interrogatories," and "depositions." Interrogatories are questions addressed to the other party that need to be answered under oath. Depositions involve recording testimony of a party or a witness. Depositions are usually used to record the parties' initial position about the facts in dispute or to record the testimony of a witness that may not be available at the trial stage.

If the parties persist, at the end of the discovery process, the lawsuit reaches the trial level.

3. The Trial Stage

At the trial level, the parties present the evidence collected during discovery to a jury or a judge. When the party has the right to a jury trial, the party must exercise it and demand a jury in the original pleading. The original pleading is either the complaint (for the plaintiff) or the answer (for the defendant)—Federal Rule of Civil Procedure 38.

Jury trials start with the selection of the jury "from a panel of potential jurors called for jury duty."[6] This process ends with the jury being impaneled.

Next the party who alleged the wrongdoing, the plaintiff—and who has the burden of proof—makes an opening statement explaining its position. The plaintiff has the burden of proof because the plaintiff has the duty to prove the statements made in the complaint—the allegations—are true.

The opposing party will answer with its own statement, and then the party who has the burden of proof will present evidence in support of its allegations. Then it will rest and the opposing party will have a chance to present its own evidence, and rest. The plaintiff offers proof in support of its allegations. This process is known as presenting the case in chief. The defendant offers its own proof and rebuts the case.

When all the evidence has been presented, the parties will have a second opportunity to make statements to the jury. The statements party make at the end of the trial are called closing arguments.

The trial ends with the judge's instructions to the jury. The judge will instruct the jury on the applicable law and, sometimes, will also summarize the evidence.

For example, for each cause of action the judge will instruct the jury as to what legal rule applies. After the judge delivers her instructions the jury retires for deliberations.

4. The Verdict

After deliberations, the jury usually brings in a verdict: "We the jury find for the plaintiff in the sum of. . . ." The jury may find

---

6 *Id.* at 826.

either for the plaintiff and award a dollar amount or for the defendant. This is called a "general verdict." Upon that verdict, the judge enters judgment. Judgment is the culmination of litigation at the trial court: it decides on matters subject to litigation.[7]

The judgment thus ends the controversy. When a money judgment is not paid voluntarily, the defendant's assets may be seized and sold to satisfy the judgment.[8]

The judgment, unless it is appealed, definitively settles the issue: it achieves *res judicata* status. This is a defense to a second lawsuit on the same claim. The English translation of the Latin's *res judicata* is "a thing adjudicated."[9]

5. The Appeal Stage

When the loosing party believes that the trial court made mistakes in applying the law, it appeals. The thumb-rule of appeal is that the prevailing party cannot appeal.

Unlike in civil law countries, in our common law system, the facts are not contested on appeal. No additional testimony is taken, nor is new evidence submitted. The opinions of the appellate courts rest on the trial record and the memoranda of law that the lawyers submit when asking for the appeal (or defending themselves against the appeal). The two basic functions of appellate courts are to review the trial court record and establish whether a reversible error occurred at the trial level.[10] Harmless errors are not grounds for appeal. Thus, "When the plaintiff has been granted all available relief, any error that the plaintiff complains of is harmless."[11]

---

7 *Id.* at 874 et seq.

8 *Id.* at 875.

9 BLACK'S LAW DICTIONARY, at 1336 (8th ed. 2004).

10 LARRY TEPLY & RALPH WHITTEN, CIVIL PROCEDURE, at 882 (2d ed. 2000).

11 *Id.* at 893.

The court of appeals' opinions are written by the assigned judge, but are filed as the opinion of the court. Usually they end the controversy (as very few reach the court of last resort, especially at the federal level) and establish the precedent for following cases. Thus, judge-made law, also known as decisional law, or case law, does not mean the totality of our court opinions. It rarely means decisions found in trial court opinions. In other words, judge-made law covers all final court decisions and is built on previous decisions through the principle of *stare decisis*, which requires courts in subsequent decisions to follow the holding in previous cases.

By now you know that case law is decisions that come from intermediary courts and the courts of last resort. Because these decisions cannot be challenged any further, they have the authority to resolve the dispute that caused them once and for all. In addition, they have the authority to regulate the future in similar circumstances. That authority rests on policies of security and certainty that are translated in law under the doctrine of *stare decisis*. Regulating the future through court decisions is a unique feature of the common law system due to its cornerstone principle—*stare decisis*.

B. CASE LAW—THE PRINCIPLE OF *STARE DECISIS*

Case law covers the opinions from appellate courts and courts of last resort. Thus, it seems reasonable to try to understand how court opinions become case law. What is the role the principle of *stare decisis* plays?

First, it should be said that this basic American legal principle comes from the royal courts of England and was received in the United States, which thus became a "common law" country as opposed to a "civil law" country—such as France or Germany—which does not formally accepts this principle of subservience to older decisions.[12] Additionally, it should be noted that the hierar-

---

[12] For a discussion of the differences between the common law and civil law system, *see* ARTHUR VON MEHREN, THE CIVIL LAW SYSTEM: AN INTRODUCTION TO THE COMPARATIVE STUDY OF LAW (2d ed. 1977)).

chical structure of the U.S. court system has fundamental implications for the degree of authority that precedent commands. The higher in the hierarchy a court is, the larger the scope of its prior decision's authority is.

The principle of *stare decisis* ensures that past judicial decisions are formally "binding" on factually similar present controversies within the same jurisdiction (a kind of geographical limitation). In other words, when a court has established a principle of law as applicable to a certain state of facts, that court and lower courts will follow that principle in all future cases in which the facts are substantially the same. Thus, the principles of *stare decisis* gives precedential value to past court decisions within well-established geographical and factual limits.

For example, a decision of the Supreme Judicial Court of Massachusetts is a precedent and so generally binding in future "like" cases in that court and the other "lower" Massachusetts courts, such as the "intermediary court" named the "Massachusetts Appeals Court,"[13] but it is not binding on any future cases arising in the courts of Georgia or California or some other state. U.S. Supreme Court decisions are not binding upon state court decisions, unless the state decisions regard a legal federal question. A federal question is an issue that regards the interpretation of a federal statute, federal regulation, or of the Constitution of the United States. A state's highest court has the last word on issues of that state's law.

1. How the Principle of *Stare Decisis* Works: Finding the Decision Within a Court Opinion

Finding the relevant case law is a very difficult process that requires years of study and later practice. This book has no ambition that it can speed up that process. Its aim is to demystify the process and points out its stages.

---

[13] A map of the Massachusetts Court System is *available at* http://www.mass.gov/courts/courtsandjudges/courts/structure_color.pdf.

The first step is to understand the source of case law: court opinions. This book will help you identify the repositories of court opinions. Once you find the court opinion you need to read you should understand that what matters is the principle of law that it stands for, and not its entirety.

A court opinion often has a very complex structure. It often confuses rather than simplifies issues. That is why we will briefly discus below how you should read a case. (See Fig. 10.)

You brief a case because you need to know what the rule issued by that court is. Thus, there are no perfect ways to do it. However, by reading court opinions, you notice that all of them have a similar structure. That structure is often found in your briefs.

1. *Heading.* Each opinion has a title and it can be identified by the reporter where it is reported. For example, *Brown v. Board of Education* (I) is the title of the Supreme Court case that covered ten appeals, one of which being the Kansas case against the Board of Education of Topeka. In the Kansas case, Brown v. Board of Education, the plaintiffs are Negro children of elementary school age residing in Topeka. They brought this action in the U.S. District Court for the District of Kansas to enjoin enforcement of a Kansas statute that permits, but does not require, cities of more than 15,000 population to maintain separate school facilities for Negro and white students.

   It is standard practice that the title of a case consists of the last name of the individual plaintiff and the last name of the individual defendant, or an abbreviation of their corporate names separated by the abbreviation "v." for the Latin word "versus," which means "against." The title of the case is always followed by the location of the opinion: the abbreviation of the compilation of opinions preceded by the volume of that compilation and followed by the page number where the opinion starts. At the end, more information regarding the year of the decision is usually added. Thus, the full citation for *Brown v. Board of Education* (I) will

Fig. 10
Finding Judge-Made Law. Briefing a Court Opinion

The only way to make sense of a case is by briefing its decision. If you need to brief your case follow the format below:[14]

1. Heading
2. Facts
3. Procedural History and Outcome
4. Legal Issue
5. Holding (the decision)
6. Reasoning
7. Separate Opinions (Dissenting opinions)

be *Brown v. Board of Education* (I), 347 U.S. 483 (1954). This means that the full opinion in Brown can be found in the 347th volume of the *United States Reports*, and it starts at page 483. The opinion was decided by the Supreme Court in 1954.

2. *Facts.* The fact of the case will help you understand the case. In *Brown v. Board of Education*, the plaintiffs, "minors of the Negro race," sought admission to the public schools of their community on a non-segregated basis.
3. *Procedural History.* Summarizing this issue helps you understand the authority of the opinion you are reading, as it tells you the court that issued it. Additionally, it helps you focus on the issues that are raised on appeal. For example, in each of the ten cases before the Supreme Court in *Brown*, other than the Delaware case,

   > a three-judge federal district court denied relief to the plaintiffs on the so-called 'separate but equal' doctrine announced by this Court in Plessy v. Ferguson [. . .]. In the Delaware case, the Supreme Court of Delaware adhered to that doctrine, but ordered that the plaintiffs

---

14 EVA H. HANKS ET AL., ELEMENTS OF LAW 81–92 (1994).

be admitted to the white schools because of their superiority to the Negro schools.[15]

4. *Legal Issues.* These are the questions of law that the court is asked to decide. In the *Brown* opinion, the court was asked to find whether segregated public schools deprived the plaintiff of the equal protection of the laws under the 14th Amendment.
5. *Holding or Decision.* The Court in Brown held that

   in the field of public education the doctrine of "separate but equal" has no place. Separate educational facilities are inherently unequal. Therefore, we hold that the plaintiffs and others similarly situated for whom the actions have been brought are, by reason of the segregation complained of, deprived of the equal protection of the laws guaranteed by the Fourteenth Amendment. [. . .] We have now announced that such segregation is a denial of the equal protection of the laws.[16]
6. *Reasoning or Dicta.* If the holding usually takes a few lines, aside from the summary of the facts, reasoning makes up the largest party of any opinion. It consists of the reasons a judge used in deciding that case in a certain way.
7. *Separate Opinions (Dissenting Opinions).* In *Brown,* there are no separate opinions. Chief Justice Warren delivered the decision of the Court.

   Of course, you may want to read a case without needing to focus on all of the aspects mentioned above. Keep in mind that you brief a case according to your own specific interests, and this is only one way in which you can read a case. It functions as an exercise in finding the decision within an opinion.

If this is the process American law school students use to deconstruct opinions and locate decisions, next let's see how, through the principle of *stare decisis,* decisions become case law.

---

15 347 U.S. 483, 487 (1954).

16 347 U.S. at 495.

2. How Does the Principle of *Stare Decisis* Work?

Case law generates rules that rely on prior decisions within the boundaries established by the doctrine of *stare decisis*. As the name "case law" suggests, a particular decision, or a collection of decisions, generates law—that is, rules of general application. Case law is sometimes used as synonym with "common law," and it covers *all* judicial decisions that have precedential effect upon later decisions from the same jurisdiction. Sometimes both terms are used to contrast with statutory law—law that is contained in the body of legislative acts. While both at the federal or state level the legislative body has the power to abolish or modify common law as it sees fit, courts have the ultimate say in deciding what a statute is.

Case law is also synonym with judge-made law. Indeed, judges "make" law when they decide a case. This is more apparent when they decide a case that is not exactly controlled by precedent or by a statute—"an issue of first impression"—and less obvious when they apply prior case law. However, either way, it is unavoidable that judges will transplant in their decisions their own understanding of the role of the law, public policy, and the mores of their times. Law is not an "antiseptic product of logic"[17] said Justice Holmes, as it is not a "brooding omnipresence in the sky."[18] Case law, Justice Holmes explained, is the result of the judges' understanding of the "necessities of the time, the prevalent moral and political theories, intuitions of public policy, avowed or unconscious, even the prejudices which judges share with their fellow-men."[19]

3. Problems with *Stare Decisis*

The principle of *stare decisis* assumes that the decision in a case should govern the decisions in all like cases that come from the

---

17 Southern Pacific Co. v. Jensen, 244 U.S. 205, 222 (1917) (dissenting).

18 *Id.*

19 JUSTICE OLIVER WENDELL HOLMES, JR., THE COMMON LAW 1–2 (1881). For a more detailed explanation, *see* WILLIAM BURNHAM, INTRODUCTION TO THE LAW AND LEGAL SYSTEM OF THE UNITED STATES. at 43 et seq.

same court or lower courts within the same jurisdiction. There are a few problems with making this principle work: (a) identifying the part of the decision that is binding, and (b) identifying the factual similar cases.

a. *The Structure of an Opinion Is a Gray Zone*

In order to solve the first problem we have to become aware of the fact that all court opinions have a complex structure. Aside from the statement summarizing the case and its procedural posture, which follow introductory elements that identify the name of the parties, attorneys, and the judge that wrote the opinion of the court, all decisions contain a description of the facts (the factual dispute), as well as a summary of the legal issues (the legal face of the dispute). Opinions thrive on their decisions (holding) and the reason on which they rest that decision. The reason given for the holding is also part of what is known as "dicta." Only the holding is binding. But how does one know what the holding is? How can one formulate the rule of law established by each case?

> The job of stating a reasonable rule of law—of predicting the decision of the court on the new facts—is not easy; it is an art rather than a science and as such is primarily a matter of feel [. . .] The key to the determination is policy. What was the policy (or policies) underlying the earlier decisions? Are there facts in the new case that raise different policy considerations? Of course, if the court believes the policy of the original decision was wrong, it may overrule it or [. . .] "confine it to its special facts."[20]

From where I stand, *stare decisis* is a myth that works. It is a legal fiction that we need in order to function as a democracy. Judges need it in order to legitimize their decisions. Justices O'Connor, Kennedy, and Souter make a magisterial use of the myth in *Casey*,

---

[20] Jane Ginsburg, Legal Methods: Cases and Materials, at 121 (2d ed. 2004).

which they present as following the rule of *stare decisis* and retaining the "essential holding of *Roe v. Wade*."[21]

The myth of *stare decisis* assumes that there is a limit, sometimes called "the painfully obvious sophistry," which will enable one to distinguish the holding or the decision of the case from the dicta of the case, and thus reliably apply the so-called "precedent." The reality is that applying the principle of *stare decisis* is a gray zone exercise where no one knows what the court will do until it decides, and only then, in hindsight, can one make the argument of *stare decisis*. Of course, its fictional nature does not negate its value. It gives us a sense of stability and order that we cherish and use.

Another aspect of the myth of *stare decisis* is that often courts are persuaded by "the sayings of learned text-writers." This discussion of the reasoning behind the decision is known as "dicta." It will often be encyclopedic, including extensive citations to and discussion of all prior relevant cases and many secondary authorities known as secondary sources, such as law review articles and treatises.

b. *Identifying the Factually Similar Cases*

In order to apply the principle of *stare decisis*, one needs to find the law that is binding. That law is the holding of all similar cases. However, similar cases may mean the facts itself were similar or the issues were similar, or even that the courts perceived them as similar despite substantial differences. For example, the plaintiff in *Roe v. Wade* was a woman who sought an abortion in Texas when Texas had a statute that prohibited abortion. In *Casey*, the plaintiff was a not-for-profit "Planned Parenthood" that challenged five Pennsylvania statutory provisions that made abortion more burdensome than before their enactment. Despite these differences, the *Casey* court stated that it relied and upheld the "essential holding in *Roe v. Wade*."

---

21 Planned Parenthood of Southeastern Pennsylvania v. Casey, 505 U.S. 833, 846 (1992).

We briefly explained above how case law works. We described how opinions are issued, and we identified them as the primary sources of case. Next we will talk about locating the appropriate case law repositories and we will touch upon a few basic techniques of finding specific case law. Finally we will talk about completing your research process and making sure that what you found is still good law.

C. REPOSITORIES OF DECISIONAL LAW OR CASE LAW

A court decision is usually included in the written opinion that marks the end of the legal dispute. Those opinions are published in book-format bound volumes called "reporters" or "case reports." Those reporters may contain cases organized chronologically by jurisdiction, or geographically, but their organization is not useful unless you know the proper citation of the case in which you are interested. The two most comprehensive fee-based databases—Lexis and Westlaw—cover most of those cases. The free-of-charge electronic databases are more limited in their coverage, as shown below.

The term "case law" generally describes appellate decisions, which are found in appellate opinions. The percentage of appellate court opinions that are published varies widely and has, in general, been declining in recent years as the number of appeals has increased. Among the federal courts of appeal, fewer than half of their decisions are published. The judges who decided the case make the decision whether to release their decision for publication.[22]

Case reporting began informally and selectively. It became more systematic when the states as well as the U.S. Supreme Court decided to start publishing their decisions in "official" reporters. The U.S. Supreme Court opinions are published in three places, one—*United States Reports*—is the official reporter published by the

---

22 WILLIAM BURNHAM, INTRODUCTION TO THE LAW AND THE LEGAL SYSTEM OF THE UNITED STATES 73–79 (3d ed. 1995).

U.S. Government Printing Office since 1790, and two commercial others. The *Supreme Court Reporter* is published by West Publishing Company, and the *Lawyer's Edition* is published by Lexis. They are all available electronically, either free-of-charge from LexisOne or for a fee from the two major electronic services Westlaw and Lexis.[23]

West Publishing Company, currently a multinational private company part of West Thomson, began compiling those cases in the 1880s.[24] Today it publishes both federal and state court opinions. It publishes the Supreme Court opinions and all federal opinions from both intermediate and trial courts. It also publishes all state court opinions from the courts of last resort in a set called the *National Reporter System.* The *National Reporter System* contains seven regional reporters. (See Fig. 11.) West has only one major corporate competitor, LexisNexis,[25] and its reporting is reserved to online access.

For the last few years, all federal courts have had their own pages available through a site maintained by the Administrative

---

[23] The Supreme Court decisions from 1991 onward are available on the Court's Web site, *at* http://www.supremecourtus.gov/.

From 1991–2001 the decisions are PDF copies of the decisions contained in the *United States Reports* (vols. 502–537).

[24] Thomson/West, *Historic Highlights, at* http://west.thomson.com/about/history/.

> In June 1996, The Thomson Corporation, a leading provider of integrated information solutions to business and professional markets worldwide, brought together the venerable businesses that composed Thomson Legal Publishing with the well-known and highly respected West Publishing Co. This merger resulted in the formation of West, the foremost provider of integrated information solutions to the U.S. legal market. Today West includes such respected names as Westlaw®, Foundation Press®, The Rutter Group and FindLaw. West launched its first online service in 1975 and remains a leader in the information technology revolution.

[25] LexisNexis Group is the global legal publishing arm of Reed Elsevier, the Anglo-Dutch world-leading publisher and information provider. *See* about LexisNexis, *at* http://www.lexisnexis.com/about/.

Fig. 11
West's National Reporter System

1. SOUTHERN REPORTER

a) Alabama	b) Florida	c) Louisiana	d) Mississippi

2. SOUTH EASTERN REPORTER

a) Georgia	b) North Carolina	c) South Carolina
d) Virginia	e) West Virginia	

3. SOUTH WESTERN REPORTER

a) Arkansas	b) Kentucky	c) Missouri
d) Tennessee	e) Texas	

4. PACIFIC REPORTER

a) Alaska	b) Arizona	c) California	d) Colorado
e) Hawaii	f) Idaho	g) Kansas	h) Montana
i) Nevada	j) New Mexico	k) Oklahoma	l) Oregon
m) Utah	n) Washington	o) Wyoming	

5. ATLANTIC REPORTER

a) Connecticut	b) Delaware	c) District of Columbia
d) Maine	e) Maryland	f) New Hampshire
g) New Jersey	h) Pennsylvania	i) Rhode Island
j) Vermont		

6. NORTH EASTERN REPORTER

a) Illinois	b) Indiana	c) Massachusetts
d) New York	e) Ohio	

7. NORTH WESTERN REPORTER

a) Iowa	b) Michigan	c) Minnesota
d) Nebraska	e) North Dakota	f) South Dakota
g) Wisconsin		

Office of the U.S. Courts on behalf of the U.S. Courts, and which functions as a clearinghouse for information from and about the judicial branch of the U.S. government. Through this Web site, http://www.uscourts.gov/, the most recent opinions of our federal judicial branch can be freely accessed.[26]

---

[26] Of course, the most developed Web site belongs to the U.S. Supreme Court, and it is *available at* http://www.supremecourtus.gov/.

The trend toward electronically free access has included state courts as well. However, the situation is more diverse at the state level, because each state has its own court system and makes its own decisions about publishing their opinions online. For example, all New York state courts have their most recent two years' opinions online available through the New York State Unified Court System, at http://www.courts.state.ny.us/courts/. Over 140,000 decisions are available dating back to 2001, for many New York Supreme Court civil cases.

According to the format in which you prefer to do your search, there are different finding aid tools. We will talk only about a few, because it is this book's aim to identify to you the ways that are accessible to all for free. We will talk about electronic ways of identifying specific cases.

D. HOW TO LOCATE SPECIFIC PRIMARY SOURCES OF CASE LAW

Opinions are available electronically from different databases and through different portals. As shown below, LexisOne,[27] which is part of Lexis, offers free access to all the reported state and federal court opinions decided in the past five years, and to the Supreme Court cases from 1790 to present, free-of-charge.[28]

Recent opinions are available also from each court's Web site, and they can be accessed either by using a specialized portal, or by doing a Google search for the specific court. For example, FindLaw, which is part of Westlaw, is a portal that directs you to those Web sites. Additionally, as further detailed below, FindLaw also covers all the Supreme Court opinions from 1893 to present.[29]

---

27 *See* http://www.lexisone.com/.

28 *See* http://www.lexisone.com/lx1/caselaw/freecaselaw?action=FCLDisplayCaseSearchForm&l1loc=L1E.

29 *See* http://www.findlaw.com/casecode/supreme.html.

If you start your case law research with a citation, use the *Bluebook* and identify the specific repository. A list of abbreviations for the reporters that cover the Supreme Court cases, the federal cases, and the state cases from the courts of the last resort is offered below. (See Fig. 12.)

Remember that any court citation will contain at least four elements: a number that will indicated the volume of the case reporter, which will precede the abbreviation of the reporter, the abbreviation of the reporter, a number that will follow the abbreviation and will indicate the page where the opinion starts, and a parenthetical. Sometimes the parenthetical will contain only the year when the case what decided. Other times, there will be more information regarding the court that issued the decision, which will help you see whether that decision is helpful from a precedential point of view. For example, the *Federal Reporter* 3rd Series (F.3d) collects court cases from all federal courts of appeal. In order to know what court issued what case, it is useful to indicate the name of the court in the parenthetical. For example, without indicating the issuing court in citing United States v. Aguilar, 295 F.3d 1018 (9th Cir. 2002) and United States v. Faulkingham, 295 F.3d 85 (1st Cir. 2001), the reader would not know in what courts each one can be raised as a precedent. The *Aguilar* decision is a precedent in the Ninth Circuit Court, which geographically includes the district courts located in California, for example, while *Faulkingham* is a precedent in the First Circuit Court, which includes the district court located in Massachusetts.[30] The Appendix to this chapter will provide you with a quick view of the geographical location of the circuit courts.

If your citation refers to a Supreme Court case, your task is fairly easy. Either one of the two free-of-charge electronic portals and databases—FindLaw or LexisOne—will prove to contain your answer. If your citation refers to any case issued within the last five years, LexisOne should be your first stop.

---

30 *See* Appendix to this chapter, http://www.uscourts.gov/images/CircuitMap.pdf.

Fig. 12
Citing Court Decisions

1. Supreme Court Reporters
   a) UNITED STATES REPORTS
      - U.S.
        - Lawrence v. Texas, 539 U.S. 558 (2003)

          vol. # abbr. pg. # (year decided)

   b) SUPREME COURT REPORTER
      - S. Ct.
        - Lawrence v. Texas, 123 S. Ct. 2472 (2003)

   c) LAWYER'S EDITION
      - L. Ed.; L. Ed. 2d
        - Lawrence v. Texas, 156 L. Ed. 2d 508 (2003)

2. Federal Court of Appeals Reporters
   FEDERAL REPORTER
      - F. F.2d, F.3d

3. Federal District Courts Reporters
   FEDERAL SUPPLEMENT
      - F. Supp., F. Supp. 2d

4. West's Regional Reporters of State Courts Opinions (West's National Reporter System)
   a) SOUTHERN REPORTER
      - So., So. 2d
   b) SOUTH EASTERN REPORTER
      - S.E., S.E.2d
   c) SOUTH WESTERN REPORTER
      - S.W., S.W.2d, S.W.3d
   d) PACIFIC REPORTER
      - P., P.2d, P.3d
   e) ATLANTIC REPORTER
      - A., A.2d
   f) NORTH EASTERN REPORTER
      - N.E., N.E.2d
   g) NORTH WESTERN REPORTER
      - N.W., N.W.2d

Similarly, if you do not have either the citation or the names of the parties, you are better off using LexisOne. For example, if you want to find the Supreme Court case that decriminalized consensual sexual relations between same sex partners, a full-text search for "sodomy" in the Supreme Court cases library on FindLaw will bring up no hits.[31]

To search LexisOne, you go to www.lexisone.com, then you log in, and choose the "Free Case Law" database. Once there, choose the keyword box, and then limit your search to the database that covers the specific court whose cases you want to search, in this instance, the Supreme Court cases. A keyword search on LexisOne will bring up the relevant case: Lawrence v. Texas, 539 U.S. 558 (2003). Such a search produced 48 results on December 1, 2004. *Lawrence* is the third result.

How do you know which case is the relevant one? Unless you have preliminarily used secondary sources, or a legal news database, you will be able to pick the seminal case. That is why you should always do a preliminary search using secondary sources and only when you have limited your options move to locate the specific primary source of case law.

Sometimes, a court's Web site is a very useful place to start locating opinions. For example, on the Supreme Court of the United States' Web site[32] you may find a list of electronic portals and databases that contain the Court's opinions,[33] the Court's recent opinions, as well as mimeographed copies of 36 volumes of the official Supreme Court Reporter, the *United States Reports*, which cover opinions decided from 1991 to 2002.[34] Furthermore, the Court's Web site also contains a "Case Citation Finder," whose purpose is

---

31 *See* http://caselaw.lp.findlaw.com/scripts/casesearch.pl?cirestriction=sodomy&court=us.

32 *See* http://www.supremecourtus.gov/.

33 *See* http://www.supremecourtus.gov/opinions/obtainopinions.pdf.

34 *See* http://www.supremecourtus.gov/opinions/boundvolumes.html.

to help searchers obtain the proper citation of a Court's opinion, when they know the name of either party.[35]

When the citation refers to an older case, you can locate the specific reporter in your public library. Reporters are cataloged in the same way books are cataloged. Once you learn their title, you type it in the appropriate title search box on the library's online catalog.

When you do not have a citation for your case, and your search is focused on a subject matter, your best approach, as often emphasized through this book, is to locate a secondary source that identifies the cases, and their citation for you. Then you proceed as stated above.

West's reporters have their own indexing tool, the digest. As mentioned earlier, using a print digest can be a difficult process. If you need to use it, start with the paper product and find the number the West editors allocated to your topic and then a second number, which is associated with a more concrete subtopic. For example, the topic number for "Charities" is "75" and the key number that identifies "charities' beneficiaries" is 35. If you choose to located cases using the paper digest, all you need to know is your topic and the "key number (k)" within your topic. However, if you want to perform your search on line, through Westlaw, you need to have both numbers in the following sequence "75k35." Of course, as both Lexis and Westlaw cover both federal and state courts opinions, if you search for "charities" and "benefit of disabled individuals" within the New York state full-text case law database, you should obtain the same results, whether you use either Lexis or Westlaw, and your results should include Matter of Altschuler, 645 N.Y.S.2d 999 (N.Y. Sup. 1996).

E. COMPLETING YOUR RESEARCH: THE U.S. LEGAL SYSTEM—A SYSTEM OF EVER-EVOLVING CASE LAW

Like any other domestic legal system, the U.S. legal system consists of norms that continue to adapt to social-economic changes and,

---

[35] *See* http://www.supremecourtus.gov/opinions/casefinder.html.

of course, to our ever-changing mores. When the source of those norms is case law, it is your final research step to make sure that that court decision is still good law. A decision is still good law when it is still binding authority over the area it is supposed to govern.

Unlike statutes, decisional law has a double role: it governs our future (like statutes) and settles past controversies between discrete parties. As any body of concrete rules, decisional law also has a limited life span that allows our democratic system to adjust to different needs of order.

For example, the Supreme Court in *Roe v. Wade*[36] held that all women had a "fundamental right" to choose to terminate their pregnancies absent a "compelling state interest."[37] The fundamental right to choose put together by the Supreme Court in *Roe v. Wade* was comprised of three components, for each trimester of pregnancy. The women had complete control over their pregnancy until viability—during their first trimester of pregnancy. Afterwards, during the following two trimesters of pregnancy, upon showing a compelling interest in the pregnancy, the state was allowed to interfere and issue different state regulation that could have adversely impacted a woman's right to decide the future of her pregnancy.

> With respect to the State's important and legitimate interest in potential life, the "compelling" point is at viability. This is so because the fetus then presumably has the capability of meaningful life outside the mother's womb. State regulation protective of fetal life after viability thus has both logical and biological justifications. If the State is interested in protecting fetal life after viability, it may go far as to proscribe abortion during that period, except when it is necessary to preserve the life or health of the mother.[38]

---

36 410 U.S. 113 (1973).

37 *See* discussion in Roe v. Wade, 410 U.S. at 155 et seq.

38 410 U.S. at 163–64.

However, the *Roe v. Wade* right to choose did not last long. The Court substantially altered it 20 years later in *Planned Parenthood of Southeastern Pennsylvania v. Casey.*[39] In its new embodiment, the woman has no absolute right to choose: states could regulate a woman's pregnancy and interfere with her own wishes before the viability point.

In *Casey*, the Court held that a woman could still terminate her pregnancy before viability,[40] whether "viability occurs at approximately 28 weeks, [or] at 23 to 24 weeks,"[41] but that she had lost her complete control over her pregnancy during that period of time. The Court allowed the state to interfere and obstruct her potential desire to abort the fetus. The only limit the Court imposed was that the state could not pass legislation that would create requirements that would likely become a "substantial obstacle to the woman's exercise of the right to choose."[42] If under *Roe*, the woman had more control, and the state's interference was more limited, under *Casey* the woman's prerogatives became less while the state's interference increased. The state could pass rules about an informed consent requirement, mandatory 24-hour waiting periods, etc., meant to discourage women from aborting.

However, remember that the Supreme Court case law is the law of the land. Supreme Court cases are open to few changes. Either the Supreme Court reverses itself,[43] as it did in *Brown v. Board of Education*, or changes its approach to an issue, as it did in *Casey*, or very rarely, Congress will enact a statute that will invalidate a Court's decision. To make sure that the decision you found is still

---

[39] 505 U.S. 833 (1992).

[40] ("The woman's right to terminate her pregnancy before viability is the most central principle of *Roe v. Wade*. It is a rule of law and a component of liberty we cannot renounce.") 505 U.S. at 871.

[41] 505 U.S. at 860.

[42] 505 U.S. at 877.

[43] For a list of subsequently overruled Supreme Court decisions, *see Supreme Court Decisions Overruled by Subsequent Decision, at* http://www.gpoaccess.gov/constitution/pdf/con041.pdf.

good law, you should try to do a keyword search the Supreme Court database in LexisOne for cases decided after the opinion you have found was decided. Similarly, when you search the validity of a federal case from a lower court, use LexisOne for cases decided both by the intermediate court of appeal and by the Supreme Court. Additionally, you should see whether there are any federal statutes issued on that topic that might change the holding of the case at hand. When you search the validity of a state court case you need to check both the state statutory compilation and the state case law. At the state level, such research becomes more tedious, and it is more feasible for a non-law student to locate a secondary source that will summarize the applicable law, and understand that its validity is as of the date of publication.

Of course, as mentioned above, if you have access to either Lexis or Westlaw, updating your search will take only a few moments. For a fee, both databases offer updating services: Lexis through Shepard's and Westlaw through KeyCite. Additionally, the limited version of Lexis, LexisNexis Academic, allows undergraduate students to update their Supreme Court case law research through Shepard's® for U.S. Supreme Court.

The next chapter will focus on the last governmental lawmaking branch: the executive branch and the administrative agencies. It will explain the two components of administrative law: administrative rules and regulations, which can be viewed as the administrative counterparts of statutory law, and administrative decisions, which can be viewed as the administrative counterpart of decisional law.

APPENDIX
THE GEOGRAPHIC MAP OF THE FEDERAL CIRCUITS

Geographic Boundaries
of United States of Appeals and United States District Courts

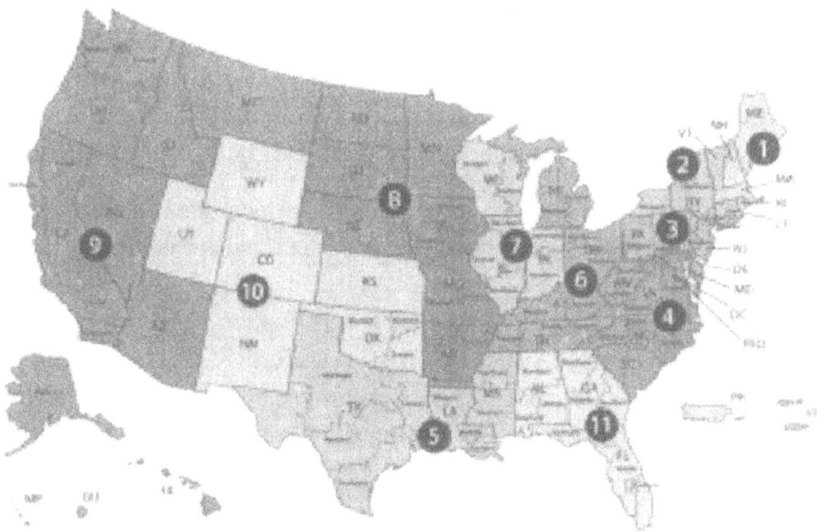

Source: http://www.uscourts.gov/images/CircuitMap.pdf.

Chapter 6
ADMINISTRATIVE LAW: WHAT IT IS, WHERE IT IS, AND HOW YOU FIND IT

A. INTRODUCTION

As in the other chapters of this book, we will first briefly describe what administrative law is and how it works so you will have a better understanding of the similarities and differences between American administrative law and this body of law within the civil law system countries, for example. Then we will talk about the appropriate repositories of administrative law, and about basic techniques of finding specific administrative provisions. Finally we will talk about completing your research process and making sure that what you found is still good law.

Article 1 of the Federal Constitution delineates the congressional legislative powers to specific socio-economic areas, such as interstate commerce. However, within those areas the congressional legislative powers are absolute. Congress can adopt all the necessary laws. It can do so directly, by enacting statutes, or indirectly, by delegating its powers to other governmental entities: federal agencies.

Why does Congress delegate its legislative powers? There are a few answers equally valid to this question. First, Congress is in session a limited number of days each year, and when in session Congress can regulate only those issues that were brought to its attention. Then, as shown in Chapter 4, there are limited ways in which Congress can initiate legislative action. Furthermore, even when it acts, Congress is not able to pass sufficiently detailed legislation that will answer all the public needs accordingly.

Today, governing is a complex process that requires detailed rules. Think about the level of detail securitie, or immigration regulations need.[1] Thus, on a regular basis, in the areas in which Congress is authorized to pass legislation, it usually delegates its regulatory powers to an agency.[2]

Congressional statutes empower federal agencies, such as the Securities Exchange Commission or the Food and Drug Administration, to deal with issues within their delegated powers in two ways: through rulemaking[3] and through adjudication. This transfer of power occurs under the delegation doctrine. This doctrine requires that that the enabling statute details the role of the regulatory agency in precise terms that will make supervision by the legislature meaningful. Aside from legislative control, agencies that have judicial powers, in addition to their legislative attributes, are also supervised by the courts, and thus open to judicial review.

Agencies develop cumbersome procedural rules that they follow during both rulemaking and adjudicatory process. However, there are some common features that they follow and they will be briefly described below.

---

1 After March 1, 2003, the Immigration and Naturalization Service (INS) has been incorporated into the Department of Homeland Security, the Directorate of Border and Transportation Security (*i.e.*, U.S. Customs and Border Protection and the U.S. Immigration and Custom Enforcement), the U.S. Citizenship and Immigration Services (USCIS), the Office of Shared Services, and the Office of Immigration Statistics.

2 For example, near "the turn of the century, agencies like the Interstate Commerce Commission and the Federal Trade Commission were created in an attempt to control the anticompetitive conduct of monopolies and powerful corporations." However, in a reverse of the original trend, new powers are given to bureaucracies in a desire to answer to create a political agenda rather than answer public demands for action and redress social problems. For a brief description of how the U.S. Citizenship and Immigration Services (USCIS) rules are made, *see* http://uscis.gov/graphics/lawsregs/regDEV.HTM.

3 The Administrative Procedure Act, § 551(4), defines a rule as an agency statement with future effect that is designed to implement or prescribe law or policy.

B. ADMINISTRATIVE RULEMAKING OR RULE PROMULGATION

Agencies are entrusted with lawmaking activities by their enabling statute. Approximately 90 federal agencies, some of them established as independent commissions and others as more or less separate branches within cabinet departments, are now involved in the regulation of business and other private activities.[4]

Usually the rulemaking process starts with a simple notice and comment process. Agencies are required by the Administrative Procedure Act to notify interested parties of the rules they intend to adopt. Those interested may send their comments about the proposed rule to the agency, and the agency is required to take them into consideration. Again, when the agency passes its final rule, it must give notice of the rule to all affected by it. In that end, the agency publishes its final rules. "Acts of Congress require publication of administrative regulations in a daily and official gazette called the Federal Register, and further require that regulations be systematically arranged and codified, by a continuing process, in the Code of Federal Regulations."[5] The date of the publication of the final rule marks the beginning of the grace period at the end of which the persons affected by the rule will be found in violation of the specific policy.

For example, Congress passed the Immigration and Nationality Act (INA in 1952).[6] Since then, Congress amended it a few times, including in 2002 through the Homeland Security Act.[7] According to their delegated powers, related agencies further developed and implemented the act and adopted specific rules.

---

4 JANE GINSBURG, LEGAL METHODS: CASES AND MATERIALS 64 (2d ed. 2004).

5 *Id.*

6 Pub. L. No. 82-414.

7 Homeland Security Act of 2002, Pub. L. No. 107-296.

More recently, under the authority of the Homeland Security Act, the Department of Homeland Security adopted an interim final rule regarding the disclosure of records and information. This rule was published on January 27, 2003. Note that although the rule became effective on the date of its publication, January 27, 2003, written comments were welcome until February 26, 2003.[8]

The rule was published in the *Federal Register* volume for 2003 (which is the 68th volume) and it started at page 4,056. Its citation thus becomes 68 Fed. Reg. 4,056.

In another example of detailed rulemaking activity, the Clean Air Act[9] authorized the Environmental Protection Agency (EPA) to regulate hazardous air pollutants. Under that authority, EPA proposed new air rules to Reduce Interstate Transport of Fine Particulate Matter and Ozone (Interstate Air Quality Rule). The rules require 29 Eastern states and the District of Columbia to reduce emissions from some pollutants.[10] The EPA published its proposed Interstate Air Quality Rule in the *Federal Register* on January 30, 2004. Because the rule was published in the *Federal Register* volume for 2004 (which is the 69th volume) and it started at page 4,566, it can be cited as 69 Fed. Reg. 4,566–4,650.[11]

The rule aims to reduce emissions of SO_2 and NO_x, which cause acid rain, by 2015. Unlike statutory provisions, administrative rules are very detailed. For example, the Interstate Air Quality Rule states that SO_2 emissions must be reduced by 3.6 million tons in 2010 (approximately 40 percent below current levels) and by another 2 million tons per year when the rules are fully imple-

---

8 *See* http://uscis.gov/lpbin/lpext.dll/inserts/dhsfr/dhsfr-2/dhsfr-1092/dhsfr-4140?f=templates&fn=document-frame.htm#dhsfr-68fr4070.

9 *See* § 112 of the Clean Air Act Amendments of 1970 at 42 U.S.C. § 7412 (2000).

10 Those pollutants are sulfur dioxide (SO2), nitrogen oxides (NOx), and mercury.

11 To view the rules, go to http://a257.g.akamaitech.net/7/257/2422/30jan20040800/edocket.access.gpo.gov/2004/pdf/04-808.pdf.

mented (approximately 70 percent below current levels). Similarly, it aims for NO_x emissions to be cut by 1.5 million tons in 2010 and 1.8 million tons annually in 2015 (about 65 percent below today's levels).[12]

In addition to their rulemaking power, administrative agencies also solve various controversies. While the procedure varies from agency to agency, there are some common elements among all agencies involved in administrative adjudication.

C. ADMINISTRATIVE ADJUDICATION

Unlike the common perception, courts are not the main instrumentalities for the disposition of controversies. More and more controversies are resolved before administrative judges, within the scope of power of various administrative agencies.

For example, in addition to its rulemaking tasks, the EPA has adjudicating functions. The Toxic Substances Control Act requires any chemical manufacturer, who learns that a product presents "a substantial risk" of health or environmental harm, to inform the EPA, and thus it delegates adjudicating authority to the EPA for all instances of corporations failing to do so.

Recently, the EPA has filed a complaint against the DuPont Corporation for failing to inform the agency about the toxic effects of a soaplike material[13] it uses to make stain- and stick-resistant surfaces and materials for a wide array of products, such as Teflon frying pans.[14] The present EPA complaint was the result of pressure by the Environmental Working Group, a private advocacy group, and by Ohio and West Virginia residents.

Administrative adjudication has grown both at the federal and state level. At the federal level, for example, adjudication takes the

---

12 *See* Interstate Air Quality Rule, Basic Information, *at* http://www.epa.gov/interstateairquality/basic.html.

13 Perfluorooctanoic acid which is also known as C-8.

14 For more on Teflon and DuPont, go to http://www.teflon.com/.

form of a trial—usually called an administrative hearing—and informal adjudication—often described as the administrative process that is neither rulemaking nor a hearing.[15] For example, when a person disputes federal retirement benefits, she will first have to raise that dispute with the Social Security Administration of the Department of Health and Human Services, which will issue an order or decision. If the aggrieved person is still unhappy with the outcome, she will seek next a court's intervention. Under the Administrative Procedure Act, all administrative decisions are subject to judicial review in courts. The scope of judicial review is limited, and it does not constitute a retrial of the case. Its scope is similar to that of judicial appeal of trial court decisions.

While many agencies announce their decisions, there is no statutory requirement for their publication similar to the statutory requirement to publish both the agency's proposed and the final rules. As shown in the next section, this creates a rather cumbersome situation for those interested in finding agency decisions. However, it should be noted that federal agencies have excellent Web sites that contain their recent rulemaking and decisional law, and both fee-based electronic services, Westlaw and Lexis, cover many of those decisions. Additionally, there are commercial publishers, such as the Commercial Clearing House (CCH), that specializes in publishing administrative decisions.

D. REPOSITORIES OF ADMINISTRATIVE LAW

Federal administrative rules and regulations, as well as executive orders and other presidential documents, are published in two official publications: The *Federal Register*, and the *Code of Federal Regulations* (C.F.R.). State administrative rules and regulations are also published in similar collections.

The *Federal Register* is the official daily publication of rules, proposed rules, and notices of federal agencies and organizations.

---

[15] WILLIAM F. FOX, JR., UNDERSTANDING ADMINISTRATIVE LAW, at 133 (2d ed. 1992).

Additionally it publishes executive orders and other presidential documents. All daily issues published in a given year constitute a single volume. Each volume is paginated consecutively.

Each year a new volume of the *Federal Register* is published. Its most recent volumes, including the current one, the 69th, are available electronically from GPO Access,[16] and through FindLaw.[17]

The *Code of Federal Regulations* republishes the general and permanent rules and organizes them by 50 broad topics, such as "Housing and Urban Development" (title 24) or "Wildlife and Fisheries" (title 50). Those topics, as mentioned before, do not necessarily correspond to those used by the U.S. Code to organize federal statutes. Thus, you cannot use your knowledge about a title of the U.S. Code to substitute for searching for the appropriate title in the C.F.R. Remember: title 34 of the C.F.R. covers copyright issues, not title 17, although it is under title 17 of the U.S. Code that you will find copyright status.

The 50 titles of the C.F.R. are issued on a quarterly basis, so that the C.F.R. is completely revised each year. Starting with its 1996 volume, the *Code of Federal Regulations* is also available electronically from GPO Access,[18] as well as through FindLaw.[19]

Usually, state administrative rules and regulations are also published chronologically and topically. A list of the title of those compilations is available in the *Bluebook*. Once you know their title, you can easily locate them in a library catalog, or online.

For example, the name of the New York chronological compilation is the *New York State Register (Register)*. It is a weekly publication and the 2004 issues—as well as a few of the 2003 issues—are

---

16 *See* http://www.gpoaccess.gov/fr/index.html.

17 *See* http://www.findlaw.com/casecode/fed_register.html and http://www.findlaw.com/casecode/cfr.html.

18 *See* http://www.gpoaccess.gov/cfr/index.html.

19 *See* http://www.findlaw.com/casecode/fed_register.html and http://www.findlaw.com/casecode/cfr.html.

electronically available free-of charge.[20] Those rules are also published in a codified compilation, the *Official Compilation of Codes, Rules & Regulations of the State of New York.* While there is no free electronic database that contains this code, parts of it that are pertinent to diverse state departments are available through that department's Web site. For example, the environmental rules and regulations are regulations are available through the Web site of the Department of Environmental Conservations.[21]

To the extent federal agencies have the authority to solve disputes, their decisions need to be recorded. The decisions issued by the U.S. Securities and Exchange Commission, for example, are available both in commercial as well as in official publications, in print—*Decisions and Reports*—and electronically. For example, the Commission's Opinions and orders issued from 1996 onward are available electronically free-of-charge from its official Web site.[22]

As mentioned before, both Lexis and Westlaw cover federal and state administrative law. Both cover the *Federal Register* from 1980 onward and the current version of *Code of Federal Regulations.* Additionally, Westlaw covers historical versions of the *Code of Federal Regulations,* from 1984 onward. Moreover, Lexis covers the officially published decisions of all state departments, and many federal agencies. Both Lexis and Westlaw cover federal decisional law reprinted in commercial publications available through them. Similarly, both Lexis and Westlaw cover state administrative rules and regulations as well.

E. HOW TO LOCATE SPECIFIC PRIMARY SOURCES OF ADMINISTRATIVE LAW

When you know the citation of the document you want to locate, you need to use the *Bluebook* to identify the appropriate repository.

---

20 *See* http://www.dos.state.ny.us/info/register/2004.htm.

21 *See* http://www.dec.state.ny.us/website/regs/.

22 *See* http://www.sec.gov/litigation/opinions.shtml.

For example, if you have the following citation, 69 Fed. Reg. 4,566–4,650, use the *Bluebook* to refresh your memory about the meaning of the citation. Thus, Fed. Reg. stands for the *Federal Register*, 69 is the (current) volume number, and the last two numbers are the page range containing the document. By going to the rule, you find that this is the proposed EPA rule regarding the Interstate Air Quality Rule published on January 30, 2004.

With that citation you can access the EPA's proposed rule both online and in print. As you know, the recent *Federal Register* volumes are available both in print and online.

Similarly, if you want to locate any proposed federal rule, the *Federal Register* is your source. Remember that the print version of the *Federal Register* has both quarterly and annual subject matter indexes, and its electronic equivalent is at the same time as searchable. For such an electronic search, you may use either the electronic portal FindLaw, or the full-text database available on GPO Access.

If your citation reads 40 C.F.R. § 1500 et seq., again, go to the *Bluebook* to refresh your memory about its meaning. Like all legal citation, this one can be easily translated also. The first number represents the title (40) where the rules have been codified, the abbreviation sends you to the codified compilation of administrative rules, the *Code of Federal Regulations*, and the section number tells you where the rules starts. Again, assuming that you want to see the current version of those rules, you can access them both in print and online. Once you locate them, you see that they regard the implementation of the National Environmental Policy Act of 1969 through the Environmental Quality Council.

When you do not know the citation to your document, you can use the index to the C.F.R. To locate the rules mentioned above, the index proves to be useful. Similarly, that search can be done on the electronic database.

For such a search, FindLaw is the right approach. Go to www.Findlaw.com and choose the "Federal and State Codes" database. Then you limit your search to the *Code of Federal Regulations*. There you can do a keyword search for "arsenic" and "water."

FindLaw is a portal to administrative law, and will automatically link you to the official electronic version of the Code, published by the Government Printing Office, and available at GPO Access. Your search will bring up the "national primary water drinking regulations" that are cited as 40 C.F.R. 141.

Presidential documents and the final rules issued by federal agencies are then published in the *Code of Federal Regulations.* For citation purposes, it is abbreviated as C.F.R.

Similarly, when you search for state administrative rules or regulations, make sure that you use the *Bluebook* and learn the name of the appropriate compilation. For example the following citation: 6 N.Y.C.R.R. § 1.25 refers to a permanent rule contained in the *Official Compilation of Codes, Rules & Regulations of the State of New York,* while a citation that mentions N.Y. St. Reg. refers to a document published in the *Register,* and which can be a notice, a proposed rule, or a final rule.

It is impossible to search for an in-print document whose citation you have unless you first locate the appropriate compilation. Furthermore, state law databases are hard to search using Boolean search strategies. They are helpful if you know the date when the rule was passed, of course, unless it is an executive order[23] or a rule available through a department's Web site[24] and they you can locate it easily by doing a mere Google search.

Searching for administrative decisions is an unpredictable exercise as well. If you have a citation to a printed reporter, once you decipher the meaning of the abbreviation, then you can easily find the title in a library catalog, and knowing the structure of any legal citation, locate the decision. For example, the following citation "Keller Ford, Inc., 336 NLRB 722" holds no mysteries once you

---

[23] If you search for "Executive Order No. 113.74: Continuing the Suspension of Certain Provisions of Law" use the Google search engine and you will obtain it without any problems; *see* http://www.dos.state.ny.us/info/register/2004/jan28/pdfs/executiveorders.pdf.

[24] For the New York rule regard deer hunting in Gilbert Lake State Park, you need to do a mere Google search, and you obtain the rule 6 N.Y.C.R.R. § 1.25.

have identified the full name behind the abbreviation "NLRB." NLRB stands for the National Labor Relations Board. The citation, which contains the name of a corporation, is likely to designate a decision. The National Labor Relations Board publishes its own reporter whose title is *Decisions and Orders of the National Labor Relations Board.* Thus, you can easily find the decision cited above if you recollect that "336" is the volume number, and 722" is the number of the page where the decision starts.

Making full use of the information you have when you start your research will help you identify the source that contains the legal norm you need. Once you have located it, you still have to go one more step. You need to make sure that your findings are still good law.

If you know the legal citation of the rule you are interested in, of course, the easiest way to locate it—as with the majority of legal citations—is to use either Lexis or Westlaw and type in the "Get a Document" or "Find" search box. Again, if you do not know it, you may use the appropriate full-text library within either Lexis or Westlaw and locate the document through a "key word" search.

F. COMPLETING YOUR RESEARCH: THE U.S. LEGAL SYSTEM—A SYSTEM OF EVER-EVOLVING ADMINISTRATIVE LAW

Administrative law is an integral part of the U.S. legal system It consists of rules, regulations, and decisions issued by agencies. These rules are issued by agencies according to clear statutory provisions that enable the agency to fill in the gaps left by a statute. Thus, administrative rules may not hold a dramatic place in the hierarchy of social order, but without them, much or our government would not be able to function.

Administrative rules have a well-defined life. From one administration to the other, rules contained in presidential executive orders are often terminated.[25] But the short life span of adminis-

25 Presidents tend to define their political agenda through executive

trative rules goes beyond those covered in executive orders. As shown below, administrative rules are often changed or replaced by the issuing agency.

For example, in *Abbott Laboratories v. Gardner*,[26] a seminal case that discusses ripeness—when a dispute is sufficiently mature to be decided in a court of law—the Court also touched upon the issue of the viability of administrative rules, when it discussed whether the administrative rule in dispute was issued in excess of the agency's authority. The Federal Food, Drug and Cosmetic Act as amended by the Drug Amendments of 1962 (FFDCA)[27] authorized the Food and Drug Administration Agency (FDA) to promulgate necessary rules to implement its provisions. The statute required manufacturers of prescription drugs to print the "established name" of the drug "prominently and in type at least half as large as that used thereon for any proprietary name."[28] The FDA acted accordingly, and issued a rule for the "efficient enforcement" of the FFDCA Act that required the established name to be used any time the proprietary name was used.

Apparently, FFDCA sought to remedy a practice, followed by pharmaceutical manufacturers, of discouraging the sale of generic drugs, by promoting brand names among health care professionals and large-scale advertising, which led to instant recognition of the brand name to the detriment of the generic drug and its manufacturers.

---

orders. For example, the decision to support an international gag rule on abortion issues on recipients of federal money had been supported by Presidents Reagan and Bush H. and Bush W., and opposed by President Clinton. *See* discussion in Dana Neacşu, *Imposing Sexual Restraint Abroad*, L. REV. MICH. ST. U. DET. C. LAW 885.

26 387 U.S. 136 (1967).

27 52 Stat. 1040 and 76 Stat. 780, 21 U.S.C. § 301 et seq.

28 This was the name given by the government, then the Secretary of Health, Education and Welfare, *see* 387 U.S. at 137–38. The proprietary name was the trade name under which its manufacturer advertised the product—its brand name.

FFDCA required manufacturers of prescription drugs to print the "established name" of the drug "prominently and in type at least half as large as that used thereon for any proprietary name."

In *Abbott Laboratories* the Supreme Court acknowledged the rule's legitimate birth—within the power allocated by statute to the agency.[29] Nevertheless, the rule[30] did not survive for long afterwards. It was subsequently amended. On paper it lasted a decade: form the original publication in the 1963 volume of the *Federal Register*,[31] through the 1974 volume of *Code of Federal Regulations*.[32]

Administrative decisions, although committed to agency discretion, are open for judicial review, and thus often know a short life span. The following example will make you aware of their frailty, but also of the transient nature of the specific norms that build our legal system as well.

In The Matter of Hearts Publications, Inc. and Los Angeles Newsboys Local Industrial Union No. 75, C.I.O., 28 NLRB 1006, the National Labor Relations Board (Board) had to decide whether full-time newsboys selling the newspapers published by Hearst Publications were entitled to the protection offered by the National Labor Relations Act (Labor Act), and thus to union representation. Hearst Publications alleged that its relationship with the newsboys was that of vendor and vendee.

The Board's primary task was to interpret the statutory definition of "employee." The Labor Act does not offer any explicit guidance in terms of categories of employment. It states that "The term 'employee' shall include any employee, and shall not be limited

---

29 For a more detailed explanation of the case, *see* WILLIAM FOX, JR., UNDERSTANDING ADMINISTRATIVE LAW, at 279 et seq. (2d ed. 1992).

30 21 C.F.R. § 1.104(g).

31 The 1964 volume of the *Code of Federal Regulations* republished it in title 21 allocated to public health issues.

32 This does not mean that there are no more rules that require manufacturers to identify the ingredients present in their drugs. *See* title 21 of the *Code of Federal Regulations.*

to the employees of a particular employer."[33] The Board reviewed the facts in the case and found that the publication (a) has "control and direction of the manner and means in which the newsboys perform their selling activities,"[34] (b) hires them by the allotment of corners and spots, (c) controls the number of papers delivered for sale daily; (d) at will discharge them, transfer them to new locations, and lay them off as disciplinary measures, and finally (e) although does not carry them on the payrolls, the newsboys " are and integral part" of the publisher's distribution system and organization.[35] The Board thus concluded that the full-time newsboys, who sold the paper at established spots, were "employees" as defined by the Labor Act, and they were entitled to collective bargaining and union representation in their relationship with Hearst Publications.

The company refused to bargain with the union, and petitioned the appropriated federal court of appeals to review the NLRB's decision. In Hearst Publications v. NLRB, 136 F.2d 608 (9th Cir. 1943), the court of appeals set aside the Board's order. It viewed the relationship between the newsboys and Hearst Publications in different terms than the Board. Based on the standards used by courts to distinguish between an employment and a mere contractual relationship, it concluded that the publisher had "at best a limited control over the activities of the newsboys inadequate to constitute it an employer,"[36] and that the newsboys did not work for wages, but for "the variance between the wholesale and retail price of the commodity he vends [the paper]."[37]

This decision was appealed to the Supreme Court, which granted *certiorari*. In *NLRB v. Hearst Publications*,[38] the Court further analyzed the relationship between the full-time newsboys and

---

33 The *National Labor Relations Act* § 2(3), *codified at* 29 U.S.C. § 152(3).

34 28 NLRB at 1023.

35 *Id.*

36 136 F.2d at 613.

37 *Id.* at 614.

38 322 U.S. 111 (1944).

Hearst Publications and reiterated that the main legal issue was whether the newsboys were employees within the statutory definition contained in the Labor Act Section 2(3). Absent an explicit definition, the Court reviewed the Board's decision primarily in light of the statute's purpose and legislative history, and then in light of the standards the Court used to distinguish between "employees" and independent contractors." The Court upheld the Board's decision and order and reversed the lower court's decision.[39] Additionally, the Court emphasized the principle of judicial deference to the agency's interpretation of the statute over which it has administering power.[40]

The new economic and policy standard used by the Court in interpreting the statute created congressional reaction. As a result, Congress passed an amendment to the Labor Act, the Labor Management Relations Act of 1947, in order to offer explicit guidance to the courts when they need to construe the term "employee." In the new version, the Labor Act states that the "The term 'employee' [. . .] shall not include any [. . .] individual having the status of an independent contractor."[41]

---

39 322 U.S. at 131–32.

> In this case the Board found that the designated newsboys work continuously and regularly, rely upon their earnings for the support of themselves and their families, and have their total wages influenced in large measure by the publishers who dictate their buying and selling prices, fix their markets and control their supply of papers. Their hours of work and their efforts on the job are supervised and to some extent prescribed by the publishers or their agents. Much of their sales equipment and advertising materials is furnished by the publishers with the intention that it be used for the publisher's benefit. Stating that 'the primary consideration in the determination of the applicability of the statutory definition is whether effectuation of the declared policy and purposes of the Act comprehend securing to the individual the rights guaranteed and protection afforded by the Act,' the Board concluded that the newsboys are employees. The record sustains the Board's findings and there is ample basis in the law for its conclusion.

40 *Id.* at 131.

41 The Labor Management Relations Act, 1947, H.R. Rep. No. 510. *See* 1947 U.S. Code Cong. Serv. 1135. *See also* 93 Cong. Rec. 6441–6442, 2 Leg.

The above example made it rather clear that any time your research evolves around administrative law, you need to check subsequent administrative rules and decisions, as well as the statutory and case law databases for provisions that amend or reverse your finding.

For any changes to existing regulations or the addition of new regulations to specific rules that you have located, go to the electronic version of the *Federal Register*, which will provide you with amendments to administrative rules that took place within that calendar year. Of course, you need to check whether the overviewing agency has given any recent interpretation to that administrative provision, and for that you may go to the agency's Web site. To make sure that there are no court decisions that affect your results, use LexisOne, and check both all federal cases and the Supreme Court cases. For potential federal statutory changes that may affect your administrative law research, follow the steps detailed in Chapter 3.

Similarly, at the state level, search the daily publication of administrative rules, if any, the states courts case law, and its statutory provisions. Unlike federal law research, state law research is more labor intensive and even more elusive. However, major public libraries will carry guides to state law research including administrative law, as collected in state print and electronic compilations.

By now you have a good idea of what the U.S. legal system is and how it works. You also know that each governmental branch makes law and you know how to search for those specific legal provisions. Furthermore, remember that all different substantive branches of law, such as commercial law, torts law, or intellectual property law are nothing more than statutory, decisional, and administrative law, and their study and research can be approached according to the same above principles.

HIST. OF THE LABOR MANAGEMENT RELATIONS ACT 1537 (1947). *See also* H.R. Rep. No. 245, 80th Cong., 1st Sess., 18, 1 LEG. HIST. OF THE LABOR MANAGEMENT RELATIONS ACT 309 (1947); H.R. Conf. Rep. No. 510, 80th Cong., 1st Sess., 32–33, 1 LEG. HIST. OF THE LABOR MANAGEMENT RELATIONS ACT 536–37 (1947).

Again, as mentioned many times here, the easiest and most reliable way to update your search is by using either Lexis or Westlaw. For a fee, both databases offer updating services: Lexis through Shepard's and Westlaw through KeyCite. However neither database offers the same reliable updating for administrative law research as it offers for statutory and case law research.

CONCLUSION: IS THIS ALL?

TV shows—"Law and Order," "Judge Judy," or "N.Y.P.D. Blue"—and even books of legal fiction answer many of the Americans' questions about law. Each, in its way, promotes a social view that supports the actual *status quo* of an ordered society. Decades of school attendance, and unrestrained consumption of popular culture, have taught the American people that their only liberty is ordered liberty,[1] and made them instinctively aware of "the problem of collective order."[2]

By now you too know the advantages and the weaknesses associated with the American law within the current postmodern society where law produces popular culture and is a product of popular culture. You also know what the U.S. legal system is, and you also know the tension between the role of the rule of law and each and every legal norms that composes the U.S. legal system.

You also have the basic techniques necessary to locate legal norms and make sure that they are still good law. You can find any legal rule you need to study.

This book introduced you to the U.S. legal realm in its untarnished abstract beauty. Law is a concept, true, which is used to ensure the current organization of any Western-styled society. Law is the foundation upon which today's societies are built: their government, family, property, inheritance system, and so forth. Emphatically, through the concept of order, we can understand how concrete rules that reside in statutes, court decisions, etc., work.

---

1 *See* Palko v. Connecticut, 302 U.S. 319 (1937).

2 Christopher Kutz, *Parliamentary Self-Government, in* 1 LEGAL AND POLITICAL PHILOSOPHY. SOCIAL, POLITICAL, & LEGAL PHILOSOPHY 39 (Enrique Villanueva ed., 2002). For more on this issue, *see* HENRY M. HART, JR., & ALBERT M. SACKS, THE LEGAL PROCESS. BASIC PROBLEMS IN THE MAKING AND APPLICATION OF LAW 1–181 (1994) (Chapter 1. An Introduction to the Nature and Function of Law).

There are many introductory law books. Most of them are quite interesting, although often limited in their point of view. They focus on reviewing the abstract world of the law (introduction to jurisprudence or theory of law), on a specific aspect of the law based on specific sources of law (what case law is and how it should be read) or on how you can find the law, by analyzing statutes, case decisions, etc. Each relies on complimentary introductory books that will explain the part of the law that they had left untouched. None has this book's organic approach to law, as they rely on and encourage an incremental approach to studying law. Such an approach is only to be expected, especially today, when all scholarly disciplines are in the midst of losing their provincial allure and structure. Interdisciplinary research and teaching seem to thrive and, with them, revising the methods and philosophy used in developing each one.[3] Unlike them, this book starts from a different premise, as it wants to give its readers a critical approach to U.S. law.

Chapters 1 and 2 explained the double meaning of law. It is an abstract atemporal human construct, known as the rule of law, but it is also concrete legal rules, because the rule of law comes to fruition through published manifestations: statutory norms, decisional law, and administrative rules, regulations or decisions.

For example, some rules lie in statutes and together are known as "statutory law" or "legislation." Statutory law is the product of people organized according to specific legal rules in federal and

---

[3] TOWARD A EUROPEAN IUS COMMUNE IN LEGAL EDUCATION AND RESEARCH 41 (Michael Faure, Jan Smits & Hildegard Schneider eds., 2004).

> [In law after] internationalization has completed its victory over Ihering's provincialism, a new challenge will be that of interdisciplinary research. Already at the present time there is much talk of interdisciplinary education and research, but traditional legal education and research remain highly mono-disciplinary. The new approach will require law faculties to give up the idea that their law students should know every single part of the main parts of the curriculum. Without doing away completely with knowledge, methods and philosophy will gain in importance.

state assemblies. Congress, at the federal level, is such an assembly, and its functioning is governed by our Constitution. Statutory law governs a large part of our lives. It establishes the life span of Mickey Mouse under the guise of copyright, and defines Indian reservations. It allows free postage for armed forces personnel and authorizes programs that encourage the consumption of fluid milk by children.

For you, it is apparent that statutory law is something everybody should be familiar with, and with patience, this book showed you the way. Statutory law is not as abstract as it sounds. It stems from statutes, and all those statutes can be easily found. Naturally, reading and applying statutes to your own research problems is another issue; this book does not pretend that you will know how to do everything by its end. You also know that understanding statutory law requires, at a minimum, understanding statutes, how they are passed, where you can locate them, and finally how they can be read.

Similarly, case law and administrative law spring from concrete sources of law. Case law mostly rests in the decisions of the U.S. Supreme Court. The nine Supreme Court Justices write opinions that cover diverse areas of our social lives. Administrative law resides in agency rules, regulations, and decisions. All these sources of law can be found, read, and then interpreted.

Further developing this process, Chapter 3 briefly pointed out the basic techniques of legal research. It emphasized the distinctions between primary sources—repositories—of law, and secondary sources. It pointed out the reasons and the ways of using each one. It hopefully brought law closer to you as it talked about the various print and online repositories of law and the ways to access them. Because it is this book's intention to ensure your unlimited access to the various forms of law, it paid distinct attention to the online repositories that can be freely accessed from any computer with Internet access. Finally, Chapter 3 finalized this ambitious project of popularizing the law without debasing it intellectually and punctuated how legal rules can be identified within those repositories.

Chapters 4 through 6 further examined law according to its specific sources: the legislative, executive, and administrative bodies. Then, they scrutinized techniques of legal research, according to each source.

On this note, it should be said that there are many ways of approaching law. It can even be tackled musically. Law is very operatic. It often spawns uncontrolled emotions supported by very little logic. (Think only about election campaigns or custody battles.) As there are many ways to start one's love affair with opera, for example: Berg's *Lulu* for the buffs of atonality, Bizet's *Carmen* for those of soft rock, or Giacomo Rossini's *Il Barbiere di Siviglia* (*The Barber of Seville*) for all musically inclined, there are many ways to start one's intellectual encounter with law.

This book wants to be the right first step in the study of law for all. It wants to cajole you into thinking about rights and duties, and discovering what they are and how you can learn about them. Hopefully, by now your legal undertakings will know only one limit: your very specific legal interests and needs. Good luck!

INDEX

www.ingramcontent.com/pod-product-compliance
Lightning Source LLC
LaVergne TN
LVHW012051011026
849162LV00017B/136
* 9 7 8 1 5 7 1 0 5 3 5 4 1 *